WHAT PROFESSIONALS W
ABOUT *TRANSFORMATIONAL EXECUTIVE COACHING*:

"Executive coaching is not for the weak of heart! *Transformational Executive Coaching* takes away the fear of failing for the coach by providing a workable model for supporting and guiding goal-oriented leaders. The Seven-Stage Model gives a roadmap that allows both the coach and the client to trust the process and focus on the important work of achieving goals. It is a wonderful tool for those coaches who want to combine a practical understanding of theory with real world experiences."

—Rebecca Sandifer, Ph.D., SPHR, ExecutiveTalk Solutions Coaching and Consulting

"Change, accountability, results, and sustainability are all outcomes that executives expect—but don't always get—from executive coaching. *Transformational Executive Coaching* introduces a seven-stage practical and replicable process for achieving those outcomes and more. Executives will like this book because of its focus on bottom-line results. It will be of interest to organizational development specialists as a guide to identify the factors that enable high performance. Most importantly, it will provide executive coaches with the tools, processes and approach to enhance their success in working with executive clients to reach and sustain their goals."

—Barry V. Bales, Ph.D., Assistant Dean of Professional Development, LBJ School of Public Affairs, University of Texas at Austin

"Ted Middelberg has taken his years of experience and education and melded them into a systems view of how executive coaches can improve the quality of their coaching. Using simple explanations, case studies, illustrative details, and a comprehensive model that demystifies the coaching process, Middelberg demonstrates how coaching helps to transform individuals and organizations into powerful synergistic partners."

—Dr. Thomas Sechrest, Professor of Human Development and Leadership, St. Edward's University

"Even the seasoned executive coach will want to read *Transformational Executive Coaching* which provides a new way of thinking about becoming an effective executive. Middelberg offers original concepts as well as the framework for delivering results and concrete steps to achieve and measure those results. Anyone with a role in improving the effectiveness of executives will want to understand this structured approach which, more than traditional methods, assures measurable progress."

—Nancy Anderson, former CEO TRADE, Inc, former General Manager, Hewlett Packard

"Dr. Middelberg's approach to feedback (interviews by the facilitator) is a significant improvement to the traditional 360 approach (standardized rating forms). Not only does it dig deeper into colleagues' perceptions, but it also offers an approach to upping the odds that developmental change will occur and take hold by having the individual's colleagues weigh in with feedback on an on-going basis."

—Bernard Liebowitz. Ph.D., Certified Master Coach, President, Liebowitz & Associates, PC

WHAT EXECUTIVES HAVE TO SAY ABOUT WORKING WITH TED MIDDELBERG:

"In the Hall of Fame for top-performing executive coaches, Ted will always stand head and shoulders above the rest for his masterful understanding of the complexities of organizational dynamics and social psychology in the workplace, and his highly evolved talent for mentoring clients through personal and professional transformations. Ted is second to none in my book."

—Jeffrey Canose, MD MHA FACHE, Executive Vice President, Texas Health Resources

"Ted has incredibly rapid and precise insight into particular leadership issues. He can dive straight to the heart of a matter and deftly help you steer your way out of it. Additionally, Ted creates a safe and fun environment for leaders to examine themselves, laugh at their mistakes, and ensure a better outcome at the next opportunity. I wouldn't want to be the leadership coach who follows Ted. His work sets a very high bar."

—Chris Paterson, CEO Sunshine State Health Plan, Centene Corporation

"Ted excels as an executive coach through a unique model that focuses on trust-based relationships, self awareness and growth. Leadership is fundamentally about aligning relevant stakeholders' commitment toward a common goal. Yet paradoxically, many executive coaches still employ dated mechanisms of collecting isolated individual data points of dubious accuracy and relevance. In contrast, Ted applies leadership techniques to executive development. Ted's use of collaborative ongoing joint engagement of relevant stakeholders to the shared goal of helping the client grow to the next level of leadership sets him apart. For anyone involved in the continuous improvement of senior executives, I highly recommend learning from Ted."

—Victor Nilson, Vice President, AT&T

"Ted is a very effective executive coach and team building facilitator. His methods and approaches are grounded from his personal work experiences, continuous learning from thought leaders and practitioners in the executive coaching industry, and hands-on experience."

—President and CEO of a joint venture of two Fortune 100 companies

"Ted has a very instinctive coaching style that puts you at ease and focuses your attention on sharpening your skill set as a leader. He has the ability to dissect challenging situations and arm you with the tools and confidence to reach new levels in leadership. He is professional, confident and a great executive resource."

—Tom Wise, CEO, Superior HealthPlan, Inc.

"Ted has the ability to see deeply into our personalities and group dynamics. He uses that insight to steer our team to exceptional cooperation in improving our performance, teamwork and effectiveness. While Ted does a great job in the technical facilitation of our meetings, it is actually in his deeper understanding of the team psychology and his ability to bring the best out in us where I most appreciate his expertise. The benefit of his open coaching and his shadow coaching, coupled with the fact that he has been working with us now for three years, is quite valuable to our company."

—Bruce Hamilton, President, Fuelco LLC

"My experience with Ted and his coaching has been a real life game changer. It's difficult to put into words what a meaningful contribution he has made in shaping (pushing/pulling/coercing) me to become the kind of leader and person that can make a difference in the world. His style and process is incredibly effective at taking current business issues and deriving lasting lessons and skill development for leading our team into the future."

—Holly Munin, CEO Texas Foster Care, Superior HealthPlan

"Ted is a master of leveraging his keen insight, educational background, and personal and professional experiences to effect meaningful leadership growth in his clients. His approach is steeped in trust based on personal relationships and focused on growth through both personal and professional self-awareness. With an upbeat personality and sense of humor, he creates an enjoyable and welcoming learning environment. Ted has a unique ability to cut to the heart of complex social and interpersonal issues, to provide deft understanding and perspective, and to effectively guide leadership growth. Ted's approach and methodology allow him to quickly become a trusted advisor and valued resource for leadership growth and development."

—Mark Smith, Senior Vice President and Chief Financial Officer, Ultra Petroleum

"Ted is not only an excellent coach/facilitator, he is an excellent role model for the very behaviors he is trying to elicit from others. Ted invested the time to get to know me as a person and as a leader. In addition to being challenging, validating, and a great listener, his deep business and financial background make him an ideal coaching resource. Ted's approach helped me to uncover and put words to some important talents and strengths I have while also pushing me out of my comfort zone to try some new approaches to leverage them more fully. The result has been a track record of business successes and confidence builders that I have used to fuel professional growth in new areas."

—Colleen Waymel, Chief Operating Officer, Empyrean

"Ted's approach to coaching makes him unique among his peers. He has the effective combination of training, education and experience and brings all of these forward in the relationship. He takes the time to understand the individual and the dynamics of the various relationships involved and then asks carefully crafted questions that challenge you and help you reach long-term solutions. He is especially effective in helping to remove emotion from difficult situations to help identify core issues. In the end, I came away with real solutions to current problems and skills that will benefit me every day, both personally and professionally."

—David Young, Sr. Vice President Finance, St. Jude Medical, US Division

"One of the many things I enjoyed about working with Ted was his "wholeness" approach. While Ted was my coach from a corporate perspective, he took the time to really get to know me as a person, my interests, etc., and looked at how who I am separate from my job interrelates to my career goals. That was different for me and refreshing."

—Kevin White, General Manager of Financial Close, Consolidation, and Reporting, Spectra Energy Corp

"Working with Ted was my first experience with an executive coach, and engaging with him took away any and all hesitations I had. After serving in executive roles for several years, I did not know how coaching would be of benefit. It took all of two 'sessions' to learn how impactful such interactions were and how much improvement was needed to sharpen my skills and live with my decisions. Ted helped me manage through onboarding, developing, and leading a new executive team and then beginning the process of a major integration of two large organizations. His probing into my thought processes, guiding me along making difficult decisions, and being a sounding board to pass insecurities and gain confidence will never be forgotten. Thankful for Ted and proud to be able to call him Coach!"

—Chris Coffey, President and CEO, Molina Healthcare of Texas

"My coaching sessions with Ted have been a life-changing and growing experience. He provides a safe, trusted space to explore and navigate complex executive-level organizational issues and business problems. He is very effective at cutting to the heart of complicated situations, creatively leveraging my personal and professional strengths, as well as identifying and helping mitigate blind spots that I never knew existed."

—Vice President of Operations Division of a Fortune 100 organization

"Ted's coaching accelerated my growth both professionally and personally. After a stakeholder interview assessment, we developed an action plan to improve my speed of decision making, develop my executive communication style, expand my network, and develop the next generation of leaders. He helped me increase my confidence and silence my inner critic, and he was always a great sounding board for the topic de jure. Ted has been an invaluable coach."

—Carlos Rangel, Senior Director of a Fortune top-ten company

WHAT COACHES HAVE TO SAY ABOUT BEING SUPERVISED BY TED

"Before working with Ted as my supervisory coach, I did not know the benefit of this type of formal relationship between coaches. I had partnered with coaches to discuss difficult situations in a de-identified format but did not know the power of Supervision for Coaches.

Ted is refreshingly direct, compassionate, and very astute at hearing patterns, gleaning underlying issues and themes, and offering new perspectives. Each time I work with him I gain insight. That insight translates to me being a better coach next time I talk with specific clients. The benefits are immediate and practical.

He helps me see things I did not because I am too close to the situation. Ted listens objectively without any judgment, and he has a wealth of coaching experience he can bring to bear. He picked up on me and my 'should' as a coach. He reframed my situation with a new light. Another skill he is good at is co-creating options.

Ted creates a safe place for learning, reinforcement, and partnership so that I can learn and continuously improve as a coach."

—Susan Shapiro, MS, PCC, Executive Leadership Coach and President, Onpoint Leadership

"What I appreciate about Ted's supervisory style is his balanced approach of challenge and encouragement. Ted always found a way to ask the one question I needed to wrestle with and allowed me to do so in a way that ultimately built my confidence in my own coaching abilities. His warmth, humor, and genuine concern for my growth was always present. Ted helped me become not only a better coach but a more thoughtful leader and professional."

—Joshua James Knightley, Associate Director, Marshall Learning and Development, USC Marshall School of Business

"I have worked with Ted as my coach supervisor for the past year. I have greatly benefited from Ted's presence and perspective. During our sessions, I have experienced Ted to be empathetic, compassionate, wise, and caring, with a depth and breadth of professional experience that allows him to bring valued perspectives to support my growth and development both as a coach and a human being. Ted has a quality of presence that is quiet and powerful, gentle and strong, and with the capacity to create safe space for all that shows up in the session and in the client's system. I highly recommend Ted as a coach supervisor, and I feel privileged to have worked with him."

—Nancy Tylim, Master Certified Coach (ICF), Certified Coach Supervisor, and Certified Mentor Coach, Nancy Tylim Leadership Development

TRANSFORMATIONAL EXECUTIVE COACHING

A RELATIONSHIP-BASED MODEL *for* SUSTAINED CHANGE

SECOND EDITION

TED MIDDELBERG, Ed.D, MBA

Published by River Grove Books
Austin, TX
www.rivergrovebooks.com

2022 Printing

Distributed by River Grove Books

For ordering information or special discounts for bulk purchases, please contact River Grove Books at PO Box 91869, Austin, TX 78709, 512.891.6100.

Design and composition by Greenleaf Book Group LLC
Cover design by Greenleaf Book Group LLC

Publisher's Cataloging-In-Publication Data
(Prepared by The Donohue Group, Inc.)

Middelberg, Ted.
Transformational executive coaching : a relationship-based model for sustained change / Ted Middelberg. -- 1st ed.

p. ; cm.

Issued also as an ebook.
ISBN: 978-1-938416-04-0

1. Executive coaching. 2. Leadership. 3. Executive ability. I. Title. II. Title: Executive coaching

HF5549.5.C53 M53 2012
658.4/092 2012945551

eBook ISBN: 978-1-938416-05-7

Second Edition

To executives who willingly put themselves on the line to raise the bar for their leadership

CONTENTS

Acknowledgments

Thanks go to the many helping hands, visible and invisible, that helped shape the ideas and reality of this second edition. Particular thanks go to Kathleen Littlepage, who enabled me to write at an active pace by keeping track of the overall organization and thematic integration, by converting early draft material into prose more pleasurable to read, and by partnering with me throughout the process with a shared commitment to an outstanding end product. Special thanks go to the support team of professional coaching colleagues who critically reviewed the two new chapters and offered invaluable insights and suggestions. My advising support team included Tom Sechrest, Lilian Abrams, Terry Hildebrandt, and Jeff Nally.

I am grateful for the formal and informal teachers who have helped me develop and breathe life into the models and concepts that form the backbone of this book. The people who influenced my thinking are too numerous to mention and range from my father, who passed along his lifelong-learner mindset, to coaches, mentors, teachers, managers, and colleagues. Four individuals have deeply influenced my coaching efficacy and my transformative process: my department chair and advisor at the University of Texas, the late Oscar Mink, who introduced me to seminal thinkers and systems concepts; my wife, Carol Middelberg, a clinical psychologist and my best friend since college, who has encouraged me to explore and understand interpersonal dynamics and continues to help me assimilate psychological concepts into my coaching practice; my therapist/master coach, Rich Armington, who has imparted a deep understanding of the potency of being engaged in a long-term reflective partnership; and my meditation facilitator, Bill Morgan, who has provided both the training and practice of mindfulness meditation that have helped me track conversations with moment-to-moment awareness.

Finally, a special acknowledgment is necessary for my many clients, the executives who have taken the risk of committing themselves to a journey of increased effectiveness. This group's steadfast commitment to excellence enabled the continuous learning and refinements in coaching that are described in this book.

Chapter One

Transformational Executive Coaching

Executive coaching has grown from being an innovative new practice in the 1990s to being an accepted practice for supporting and developing executives. Not so long ago, a *Harvard Business Review* article referred to the wide variety of practices that laid claim to the loosely defined field of coaching as "The Wild West of Executive Coaching."[1] Since then, executive coaching has matured and been accepted as a best practice for executive and management development. The use of coaches to guide executives across the gamut of leadership challenges continues to expand unabated, growing at an estimated 40% per year.[2] One study found that almost two out of three organizations expected to increase their use of coaching over the next five years; another study found that almost 80% of the surveyed organizations used coaches.[3] This increased reliance on coaching places an even greater burden on those of us in the coaching field to improve the effectiveness of our practices through continued learning.

The genesis of Transformational Executive Coaching was my search for what executive coaches do that really matters. What actually inspires executives to make sustained change? How can coaches help leaders build their toolkit in ways that support organizational and personal success?

Over my years as a coach, I evolved from helping clients make targeted behavioral changes (such as enhancing listening skills) to helping them develop skills to identify and gather information on which problems needed to be solved. This comprehensive approach developed from my desire to increase the long-term impact of these coaching engagements, which were a considerable investment of the executive's time and the organization's resources. I focused my efforts on creating an environment that supports learning new skills and understanding how to apply those skills to future challenges. This new approach refocused my coaching process from one of "whack-a-mole" or "let's get rid of this problem" to the development of skills that enable executives to transform themselves and their environment. Executives are expected to have the ability to evolve quickly to meet the increasing complexity, ambiguity, and pace of change in their work environments—in other words, to transform as needed.[4]

Transformational Executive Coaching aims to increase the efficacy of executive coaching in order to help executives meet these expectations by:

- Generating better results
- Realizing those results faster

- Ensuring the sustainability of those results
- Building coaches' skills and capabilities

GENERATING BETTER RESULTS

All executives are driven to achieve results. Just maintaining one's current role, much less advancing to a higher level of responsibility, requires achieving results day in and day out. Effective leadership includes other factors, but the sine qua non for success is getting results. As one client put it, "I don't get to play tomorrow if I don't deliver results today." At the heart of Transformational Executive Coaching is the Seven-Stage Model, a coaching method. The Seven-Stage Model is focused tightly on the goals that are identified by the executive as being most important for personal and organizational success. The model includes specific techniques to identify the changes in behavior that will have the greatest impact on achieving those goals. One of the unique tools is a revolutionary and cost-effective feedback-gathering process employed to obtain actionable information relevant to specific goals. In addition to producing more usable information early on in the coaching conversation, the feedback methodology supports the client's change efforts during and after the formal coaching engagement.

Focusing on the quality of the feedback and consequently improving the quality of the feedback environment added a unique and powerful dimension to my clients' experiences. The concept of a feedback environment is new to many executives. Every organizational culture includes a feedback environment made up of the day-to-day availability and usability of job performance information. It encompasses perceptual concerns about the source, quality, and availability of feedback as well as how it is delivered and whether seeking it is promoted.[5] I discovered the potency of the feedback environment first as a graduate student doing research and then experientially as a coach. As a practitioner who values research, I interview my clients at the completion of the coaching engagement to assess the impact of our work. (See Appendix D: Evidence-Based Coaching Evaluation.) When I experimented with introducing the feedback-gathering methodology detailed in this book, there was a marked jump in how clients rated their outcomes.

REALIZING RESULTS FASTER

Whether an executive is trying to assimilate into a new role, grow in an existing role, or just keep pace with a dynamic and competitive environment, the scarcest resource is time. Simply put, there is never enough of it. Many traditional models of coaching begin with the process of gathering survey data from multiple people who rate the client across a range of leadership domains and competencies. These survey instruments are known as multisource feedback or 360-degree feedback, so named because input is collected from the recipient's direct reports, colleagues, bosses, and sometimes even external customers or vendors. The survey results guide the coach in identifying the issues to be addressed with the client. One of my early learnings as a coach was that techniques that were effective with managers were not necessarily the best for clients at the executive level. I found that executives already had a wealth of information about their leadership skills, so administering the traditional multisource feedback instrument was not a good use of our coaching time. The goal-setting process detailed in this book is tailored to executives and gets to the core issues faster. When I combined this goal-setting process with the cost-effective methodology for gathering robust feedback, I began spending more of the valuable coaching time working the issues and reinforcing the practice of new behaviors.

ENSURING SUSTAINABLE RESULTS

Coaching is fundamentally about change. Chapter 2 explains the Hierarchy of Sustained Change, the basis for achieving and maintaining change through Transformational Executive Coaching. One of the great challenges with all change initiatives, personal and organizational, is the tendency to backslide. Executives have the added challenge of the rapidly evolving nature of today's organizations. A unique aspect of the Seven-Stage Model is that it identifies executives' specific behaviors that support or undermine achieving their current goals while also providing them with the tools to meet future challenges.

BUILDING COACHES' SKILLS AND CAPABILITIES

It is a well-accepted tenet that we all benefit from challenging ourselves and receiving feedback on how we perform. The acceptance of the coach receiving ongoing feedback through trusted others, particularly through supervision, is a relatively new phenomenon in the United States.[6] Chapter 7 focuses on four pathways for getting that ongoing feedback. Chapter 8 provides a decision-making model,[7] along with case examples, to guide the coach across the ethical conundrums that we and our clients find ourselves in.

WHAT TO EXPECT

While Transformational Executive Coaching (TEC) is designed to guide and support coaches as they raise the bar of executive coaching, it is also useful for human resources and organizational development leaders who select coaching programs, for executives who want to understand the additional value they can receive through a transformational model of executive coaching, and for organizational leaders who are responsible for the development of their executive leadership pool.

This book is structured to provide what, how, and why: what to do, how to do it, and why it is done. It is designed to facilitate the transfer of knowledge in a user-friendly way. Two familiar metaphors capture what happens when something eventful takes place but the process is hidden. From the Wizard of Oz, there is the wizard behind the curtain who dazzles with impressive theatrics but possesses questionable substance. From the swan floating gracefully across the water, there is the image of effortless progress on the surface while the less-than-attractive activity below the water is invisible. This book includes what is going on behind the curtain and beneath the water line in the coaching process.

The ensuing chapters include detailed information on the following:

1. The theories and applied research that underpin how the coaching model achieves sustained change
2. The seven stages of the coaching model
3. Processes used to implement the stages
4. Coaching skills required to execute the model successfully
5. Templates used to guide and track progress during the coaching engagement
6. An instrument employed to verify evidence-based results

FOUNDATIONAL BELIEFS

The transformation the executive experiences through the coaching process is the move from a work environment with inconsistent levels of safety, trust, and feedback to a work environment marked by improved relationships with team members who experience an increased sense of safety and trust and who give and receive valuable feedback. The skills the executive develops in order to make this shift transcend the specific coaching engagement and become an integral part of the executive's toolkit for continued growth and development.

TEC is described as a relationship-based model for achieving sustained change because the high-quality information that informs the change efforts comes from both the coach-executive relationship and the relationships that are built within the organization. The relationship building begins between the coach and the executive and evolves as the executive extends these skills to his team and organization. The change is sustainable because the executive learns a precisely outlined feedback gathering skill. At the most general level, executives embrace this coaching as a means to increase their leadership effectiveness by identifying their most important goals and by adapting their behaviors in a sustainable way to deliver evidence-based results.

TEC is grounded on five foundational beliefs:

> Foundational Belief One: People will respond positively to the invitation to provide owned (non-anonymous) feedback to the executive on specific issues when the coach provides a carefully designed process for obtaining and giving that feedback.

> Foundational Belief Two: The owned feedback provided through this process is relevant and useful to the executive both because it is in response to a self-selected and tightly focused issue and because the executive has the ability to contextualize and further explore the meaning of feedback that is not anonymous.
>
> Foundational Belief Three: This open feedback-gathering process improves the relationships of the participants by increasing trust, reducing perceived power imbalances, and providing a foundation for discussing challenging issues; consequently, it enriches the feedback environment.
>
> Foundational Belief Four: Teaching an executive how to seek feedback around specific goals gives the executive a powerful tool for getting the best information about future challenges. Successful executives are continuous learners, and they benefit from interventions that provide them with tools to build skills that serve them long after the engagement is completed.
>
> Foundational Belief Five: Successful coaches are continuous learners who take proactive steps to get the feedback and have the reflection space they need for professional growth and development.

My passion for leadership development was an unforeseen evolution of my career. I started as a finance guy. I earned a BA in economics, an MBA with a major in finance, went on to become a Certified Management Accountant (CMA), served as VP of Finance at two organizations, and was president of the local Financial Executives Institute (FEI) chapter. As I progressed in my field, I found the issues involved in developing leaders and increasing efficiencies through people more salient and compelling. I noticed that employees and colleagues were consulting me on issues of leadership, interpersonal effectiveness, team conflict, and cross-departmental collaboration as frequently as on strategic planning or budget control.

I succumbed fully to the pull to refocus my career when I entered the doctoral program in leadership and development at the University of Texas. It allowed me to immerse myself in the theory and practice of leadership and fed my growing interest in the importance of providing valid and usable feedback. Across the span of the last thirty years, I have coordinated leadership development at AMD, coached leaders across many industries, and taught leadership topics at the graduate level.

My ongoing fascination with leadership research, theory, and practice has led me to continually learn from others in the field and to make adaptations based on my experience as a certified coach, a professor, a consultant, and a certified coach supervisor. I find I need to stay ever mindful of the theories that inform my practices in order to coach effectively and continually improve my techniques. In this spirit, I developed the grounded theory (the Hierarchy of Sustained Change) that underpins the practical coaching techniques (the Seven-Stage Model) presented in the following chapters.

Chapter Two

The Hierarchy of Sustained Change

The Hierarchy of Sustained Change consists of multiple theories and best practices on how an individual can make change in order to reach a goal and then sustain that progress. The Hierarchy posits that sustained change is the culmination of a safe and trusting environment that supports authentic relationships and expands feedback opportunities, which in turn provide the quality information that the individual can contextualize by thinking in systems. The entire process moves the executive toward the goal of making changes that are critical to achieving stated goals.

The following diagram illustrates the interconnectedness of these concepts and places them in a hierarchy of five consecutive levels.

FIGURE 1: THE HIERARCHY OF SUSTAINED CHANGE

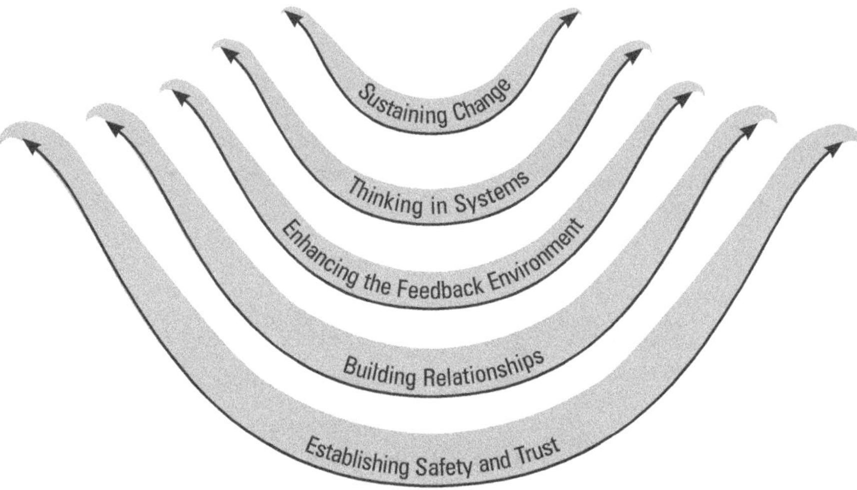

Level One: Establishing Safety and Trust

Goal: Replace defensive thinking with reflective thinking by establishing a holding environment of safety and trust.

Level Two: Building Relationships

Goal: Replace risk avoidance with the willingness to share what is important by building relationships.

Level Three: Enhancing the Feedback Environment

Goal: Replace impoverished information with the best available thinking by enhancing the feedback environment.

Level Four: Thinking in Systems

Goal: Replace *du jour* attempts to change with choices based on understanding the system as a whole.

Level Five: Sustaining Change

Goal: Strengthen individual efforts with reinforcement from a supportive system to sustain change.

LEVEL ONE: ESTABLISHING SAFETY AND TRUST

Goal: Replace defensive thinking with reflective thinking by establishing a holding environment of safety and trust.

Holding environment, a term drawn from developmental psychology, refers to a "safe place" for people to talk openly about the challenges they face.[1] Within the Hierarchy of Sustained Change, this holding environment manifests the potential, the kinetic energy in the system for change.

All of us have encountered issues of safety and trust—or the lack thereof—in our work experience. Trust is a precondition for a sense of safety. When we do not trust someone, for whatever reason, we are hard pressed to feel safe in our interactions. Not having trust that we are going to be okay makes us anxious for our own well-being and undermines the motivation to take actions that may be in the organization's best interest but that may involve perceived personal risks.

Working at the melting pot of SEMATECH proved to be a seminal learning experience for me on how safety and trust impact behaviors. Congress had just authorized the creation of SEMATECH, a consortium of semiconductor companies (SEmiconductor MAnufacturing TECHnology) formed in 1987, in order to legally allow firms to share nonproprietary competitive information in service to rebuilding the semiconductor industry and protecting both jobs and technology from going to other countries. The staff included employees from the dozen member companies who were on loan for two- to three-year assignments. The result was that fierce competitors were asked to collaborate, creating an environment rife with issues of trust and openness. As a member of the organizational development staff, I dived into the research on building trust and its importance to team performance. As

Patrick Lencioni noted in *The Five Dysfunctions of a Team*, "In the context of building a team, trust is the confidence among members that their peers' intentions are good and that there is no reason to be protective or careful around the group."[2] In essence, team members get comfortable with being vulnerable with one another and get down to work.

Around the time that SEMATECH was formed, Francis Fukuyama published *Trust: The Social Virtues and the Creation of Prosperity*, which was a perfect fit for what we were trying to achieve at SEMATECH.[3] As Fukuyama correlated economic success with the social structures that support or inhibit trust, he established that trust was more than just a feel-good aspect of organizational culture. A highly popular book, *The Speed of Trust* by Stephen Covey, continues to strengthen the linkage between trust and economic outcomes, such as time and money.[4] The formula Covey proposes is, "When trust goes up, speed will also go up and costs will go down."[5] He holds that the inverse is also true, "When trust goes down, speed will also go down and costs will go up."[6] His example of air travel after 9/11 captures this formula well. As trust went down, we all experienced additional delays and inconveniences (reduced speed) and higher air fares and loss of personal time (increased costs).

When designing interventions to increase trust at SEMATECH, we used safety-building concepts such as:

- Increasing vulnerability gradually by taking small steps and testing for reciprocity
- Clarifying roles and responsibilities
- Leveraging the competencies of the participants

- Discussing tough issues openly
- Managing boundaries
- Focusing on the integrity of the intent

We used active facilitation at meetings to ensure that positive steps were not canceled by subsequent events. We did not have the time for "two steps forward followed by one step back." As facilitators, we observed the increased willingness to take the risk of sharing and the reduction in the use of various defense strategies, such as hijacking the agenda, refusing to agree with or join speakers even on valid points, and cleverly disguising insults as humor. Over a six-month period, the team members began to recognize and acknowledge the increased sense of safety.

The dark side or shadow side of trust and safety is what happens when those attributes are absent, when we do not feel safe. Chris Argyris and Donald Schön developed several highly regarded models of thinking with a core assumption that typical organizations are characterized by systems that support behaviors aimed at avoiding embarrassment or mitigating threats.[7] Lee Bolman and Terence Deal in *Reframing Organizations*, their classic book on organizational behavior, go further and portray organizations as dangerous places where you have to look out for yourself or someone else will do you in.[8]

They (Lee Bolman and Terry Deal) translate how the behaviors identified in the models of Argyris and Schön manifest when a problem arises in the absence of trust and safety:

- "Assume that the problem is caused by the other side."
- "Develop a private, unilateral diagnosis and solution."

- "Since the other person is the cause of the problem, get that person to change."
- "If the other person resists or becomes defensive, it just confirms that the other person caused the problem."
- "Respond to resistance through some combination of intensifying pressure and protecting yourself or rejecting the other person."
- "If your efforts are unsuccessful or less successful than hoped, it is the other person's fault."[9]

Understanding these tendencies is pertinent to making changes because the distortion in our thinking when we are not operating in an environment marked by safety and trust generates misinformation. In *The Trouble with Thinking*, Lauren Powers also builds on Argyris and Schön to delightfully illustrate the cycle that follows when we start from a scary place rather than from an open, trusting place.[10]

What Powers labels the "Rat Brain Loop" is composed of four parts:[11]

Part I: Selecting information that supports what you already believe

Part II: Defining meaning from a scary place

Part III: Attaching labels that belittle you and others

Part IV: Acting or reacting to defend yourself and prove others wrong

Powers uses stories and humor in ways that make it hard to maintain a defensive posture and insist that this behavioral pattern applies to the other rat brains, "not me."

The need for undistorted reflective thinking applies to every aspect of the decision-making process. In works from the nascent and seminal writers on reflection and adult learning[12] to works by the more contemporary authors like David Clutterbuck, Julie Hay, and Elaine Cox,[13] the importance and value of reflective thinking for growth and development has been underscored again and again. As Lucy West and Mike Milan put it, "The . . . coaching task is to create the conditions for reflective thinking."[14] The Hierarchy of Sustained Change supports the coach in building the right conditions for reflective thinking and, ultimately, sustained change. My own experiences and those of colleagues consistently identify a key value of coaching as giving the executives the time and space for reflective thinking. A recent survey from coaches who have been supervised points to this same benefit.[15]

When we solicit feedback, we want the data to come from an undistorted thinking process, one based on conscious reasoning rather than unconscious mental models[16] and projections. When we use that feedback, we also want our conclusions to come from an undistorted, conscious, and analytical process. Establishing safety and trust creates the holding environment that allows us to advance through the remaining levels in the Hierarchy of Sustained Change.

LEVEL TWO: BUILDING RELATIONSHIPS

Goal: Replace risk avoidance with the willingness to share what is important by building relationships.

Establishing the atmosphere of safety and trust affords the opportunity to build relationships that can sustain the heavy lifting of sharing and reflecting on what is important. The research in the feedback field is replete with cautions on the risks of giving feedback.[17] When I trained managers on the requisite skills for providing effective performance feedback, most participants had some visceral memory of how giving feedback went badly awry despite their good intentions. Most of us have not been taught how to give feedback in a way that effectively results in behavioral changes. Correspondingly, we usually do not learn how to ask for feedback in a way that provides the insights we need to make changes. The dysfunctional manager who does not want to hear anything that implies any personal shortcomings is a familiar character. As one client phrased it, "We work awfully hard here to hide our weaknesses." However, executives who understand the value of continual improvement, no matter how successful they are, want and need feedback from others to increase self-awareness, an attribute that is strongly associated with leadership effectiveness[18] and an anchor point in emotional intelligence.[19]

Doctor Atul Gawande wrote a compelling article in the *New Yorker* on the impact coaching had on his surgical skills.[20] Gawande was an accomplished surgeon whose complication rate was well below the national average; nonetheless, he was frustrated when he reached a plateau and was unable to continue lowering his rate of incidents. He convinced a retired surgeon and teacher to observe his operations and make suggestions on his techniques. His former teacher frequently proposed small changes that combined to make a big difference, such as changing the way the surgical drape was placed to give the assistant a better reach and being conscious of how his elbow tended to rise at a certain point in the procedure. Dr. Gawande was surprised by the opportunities for further improvement and increased medical efficacy that were uncovered by the objective feedback from this trusted, knowledgeable colleague.

A significant number of my executive clients complain that the higher they rise in the organization, the harder it is to get the useable feedback they need. As Argyris put it, you need to know what people won't tell you.[21] One CEO complained that her staff just seemed to go along with everything she said. A chairman worried that the executives in the finance group were not hearing essential information from their staff. A Fortune 100 corporate officer giving mentoring advice to a new VP warned which staff members were likely to just echo his own thinking. The list goes on.

The relationship between the person giving and the person receiving feedback matters. It influences the ability to be receptive and the ability to offer authentic feedback, as well as judgments on the importance and usefulness of the feedback.[22] The perils of succumbing to someone who says, "I really want your honest feedback" are well known to most of us, from both personal and work experiences. One client shared how he made that mistake with his boss. When I interviewed the boss, he described how my client had shown poor judgment in being offensively blunt. When I asked my client how that happened, he disclosed that his boss cajoled him into a false sense of openness and inquiry. Direct reports and colleagues willing to provide candid feedback make themselves vulnerable to creating ill will, challenge, or even retribution.

On the other side, executives asking for feedback take the risk of disclosing goals that are especially salient to their success or of exposing areas they perceive to be weaknesses. They also risk being judged as uncertain or insecure.[23] Ironically, while this risk keeps executives from actively seeking feedback, the reality is that exposing oneself by seeking feedback that might be negative increases constituents' opinions of the leader's overall effectiveness.[24]

The two-way street of feedback is plagued by risks on both sides. It is precisely these risks that make developing safety and trust through relationship so significant. The importance of the relationship between a manager and direct reports is demonstrated by the fact that the relationship is consistently found to be one of the strongest influences on satisfaction in the work environment.

One of the leadership theories that best describes work environments centers on the relationship between the leader and the subordinate. Leader-Member Exchange (LMX) theory recognizes that managers develop unique relationships with direct reports and other members of the organization.[25] These relationships influence executive risk-taking behaviors, ranging from deciding which employees get which assignments and promotional opportunities to the reciprocated feedback process.[26] Better things happen to members with high-quality relationships with their manager. Research on the favorable impacts of environments with a high level of Leader-Member Exchange includes job performance, organizational commitment, job climate, innovation, organizational citizenship behavior, empowerment, and career progress.[27] The opposite holds true as well. One of the most common reasons people provide for leaving an organization is the relationship with their manager.

The importance of the executive building relationships with team members and within the organization is strengthened by new research in neurophysiology and attribution theory. Recent research by Stephen Porges in the field of neurophysiology applied to social engagement explains how a perceived lack of safety can push us past fight/flight responses all the way to immobilization.[28] We are hard-wired to engage and to constantly, though often subconsciously, test the environment for signals of risk. This contemporary research supports the models developed decades ago by Argyris and Schön. The neurophysiology research has determined that, as part of our social engagement system, we assess for safety before we selectively turn off our defenses.

This aligns with my own research,[29] leadership experience, and coaching observations. Leaders who create work environments marked by high levels of safety and trust are more likely to have members who have replaced defensive routines with openness, curiosity, and a willingness to make themselves vulnerable and to take the risk of deeply reflecting on their choice of behaviors.

The growing awareness of the importance of relationship to effective leadership has spurred new research on attribution theory, which addresses whether someone points to internal or external reasons when explaining why things go right or wrong. A new perspective provides a third alternative, pointing to the relationship involved. In a recent article detailing this approach, the authors provide a great example of what this looks like. The employee who did not get a positive performance review could explain this outcome from an internal attribution ("I did not put in enough effort") or from an external attribution ("My boss is incompetent") or from a relationship attribution ("My boss and I do not have a positive relationship").[30]

More and more evidence that the quality of relationships matters—relationships with both direct reports and others—is being gathered in the business field. As one client noted, the pivotal thing for him to do in order to reach the next level is to develop relationships with leaders at that level in the organization. This is especially significant at the executive and corporate officer level, where building alliances and working across the organization places a premium on supportive relationships.

Relationships matter because they expand the basis for safety and trust, which in turn enables others to take the risks of being vulnerable and of sharing information that might be hard to hear. If an executive truly wants to gather the feedback necessary to guide the changes that will have positive career and organizational impact, building relationships is foundational. Additional benefits of networking have been noted to include (1) helping the executive get ideas and projects more readily and easily accepted because of the goodwill established earlier, and (2) making it easier for executives to get this done across the silos of any organization.

LEVEL THREE: ENHANCING THE FEEDBACK ENVIRONMENT

Goal: Replace impoverished information with the best available thinking by enhancing the feedback environment.

My research in the late 1990s found that the pool of available and usable feedback was a critical variable in explaining the differing levels of team performance. Every organizational culture includes a feedback environment made up of the day-to-day availability and usability of job-performance information. It encompasses perceptual concerns such as the credibility of the source, the quality of the feedback, its availability, how it is delivered, and whether seeking it is promoted.[31]

My experiences as an executive coach and consultant have strengthened my beliefs that:

- Leaders strongly influence the quality of the feedback environment
- Teams with enhanced levels of available and usable feedback will outperform teams that operate in a more impoverished feedback environment

This recognition of the importance of the feedback we offer each other has been a guiding influence on my work as an executive coach. All coaching engagements are highly dependent on the quality of the feedback shared between the coach and client, as well as the quality of the feedback that the client receives from others. The most commonly used formal method for providing feedback from others is known as multisource feedback or 360-degree feedback.

Over the past two decades, I have had the opportunity to use many different 360-degree feedback assessment instruments, including two that I was involved in designing and validating. While at IBM, as part of the organizational development consulting group, I worked with leaders on interpreting their 360-degree feedback results and developing improvement plans. As a member of the worldwide team that developed IBM's Executive Competency Model, I got to review the leadership competency models at many of the best companies and to participate in developing a validated competency model. Model validation means there was independent verification that the higher-rated leaders received higher scores and the lower-rated leaders received lower scores. In turn, the competency model provided the foundation for the questions asked in the 360-degree instrument. This deep immersion in the underlying assumptions that anchor 360-degree assessment instruments was foundational to my creation of a uniquely different model for obtaining relevant, high-quality feedback.

Through my immersion in the theory and practice of building leadership competency models, the hands-on development of a highly integrated leadership development system, and the use of sophisticated analytics, I gained a deep appreciation for the strengths and weaknesses of 360-degree feedback instruments. While traditional 360-degree feedback surveys may be appropriate for many types of coaching, the feedback-gathering process advanced in the Seven-Stage Model is significantly different and is tailored to the executive level of coaching.

The use of 360-degree feedback surveys exploded throughout the 1990s as a cost-effective means to obtain feedback that otherwise was not believed to be available. Certain shortcomings have been accepted, such as the weaknesses of using generic competencies and getting feedback that is not behaviorally anchored. Certain assumptions have been unchallenged, such as the beliefs that trust is too low to get "owned" feedback and that people will share what needs to be heard. Certain unintended consequences have been ignored, such as getting results that do not guide actions or even undermine building better relationships. The technique for gathering usable feedback detailed in the Seven-Stage Model addresses those shortcomings, assumptions, and unintended consequences. Most important, the process creates a generative loop that reinforces trust and open communication, setting the stage for ongoing feedback that makes the best information and resources available to support executive decision making.

Seasoned executives often find limited value in participating in their organization's 360-degree feedback process. My clients have shared their experiences with participants who did not trust the process (fearing that the results would be used in a performance review) or who did not trust that the process was truly confidential (fearing retribution based on comments attributed to the individual). Similarly, they did not trust the intentions of some participants (suspecting contaminated data from someone with an axe to grind), or, having gotten valid feedback, they did not have the internal resources to know how to take action.

My personal experience at a well-known Fortune 500 firm demonstrates how fragile the commodity of trust truly is and how easily the feedback environment can be damaged. In my role coordinating leadership development, management at one of the larger facilities agreed to have all of the leaders participate in an anonymous 360-degree feedback process for developmental purposes. The results went to the individual leaders to use for their personal development and deliberately were not shared with the participants' supervisors or the human resources department to be used for evaluative purposes. With this condition in place, we had almost 100% participation and received many candid ratings.

When the high-tech industry hit an economic dip, the company needed to reduce their work force. Fairness and good management practices suggested that they also had to reduce the number of managers. At that point, the facility leadership insisted that they be given access to the 360-degree feedback reports, as an additional resource to help them determine whom to layoff. From one perspective, this makes perfect sense: managers want the best available information to make decisions. While understanding the desire to have data to better inform the tough choices that loomed, I countered with arguments that this violated the agreement under which people participated in the process and that it could poison the well and doom any future effort to conduct a 360-degree feedback process. I also built the case that employees and middle managers would become skeptical and not trust their leaders. These dire predictions proved to be all too true. Even though the arguments were successful, the fallout was a loss of efficiency and effectiveness due to ongoing mistrust in the executive leadership team.

The potential unintended consequences of events that undermine trust mandate that we stay ever vigilant for actions that could send an equivocal message about trust. When we see our leaders adopting a process that undermines trust, our hard-wired drive for safety makes it highly unlikely that we will be able to convince ourselves that it was a unique situation rather than a pattern.

The feedback environment consists of:

- The credibility of the source
- The quality of the feedback
- The availability of feedback
- How feedback is delivered
- How much feedback seeking there is

The feedback environment is highly influenced by the consistency of these formal and informal messages on how feedback is valued and honored as a gift. The feedback environment, while fragile, is an expandable resource, similar to employee goodwill and trust. As with all features of an organization's culture, the feedback environment reflects the culmination of the behaviors that are rewarded and discouraged. The executive sets the tone and builds the feedback environment at every level of interaction—individual, team, department, division, and corporate.

LEVEL FOUR: THINKING IN SYSTEMS

Goal: Replace *du jour* attempts to change with choices based on understanding the system as a whole.

Identifying the right things to work on requires that the right questions are asked in order to understand the system. With the right information, the changes that have the greatest impact on goal achievement can be targeted. The underlying principle is that focusing on the right goals or change efforts intensifies the energy available in the individual and the system to effect sustained change. The systemic approach offered here is built on multi-stakeholder analysis, where the issues are considered from differing perspectives. Then, with the clarity derived from each of those perspectives, a systemic view begins to emerge.

Once goals have been forged by considering multiple perspectives, the next step in thinking in systems is to organize information in ways that increase understanding of both the motivators and the barriers to goal achievement. In graduate school, I learned about an elegant approach to understanding issues of change, developed by Kurt Lewin, called a "force field."[32] One of the preeminent social psychologists of his era, Lewin looked at goal achievement as a system of balancing forces that both drive and restrain behavior. A visual aid for understanding a force field is the image of someone holding his hands together in front of him, as if in prayer. Metaphorically, the right hand is the leader pushing change, driving the process. The left hand is the organization, which softens and yields as the leader increases the pressure for change. Typically, when the leader relaxes and breathes, the left hand gently goes back to its original position. The entire system reverts to the pre-change position of homeostasis.

There are driving forces that support goal achievement and restraining forces that get in the way of goal achievement. When the leader just pushes harder, rather than addressing the restraining forces, the elements in the system that resist the changes will wipe out any short-term gains. Understanding the system of driving and restraining forces that are at play reveals the areas to pinpoint for intervention or focus.

This concept applied to specific targeted coaching goals creates the path of maximum speed to change. First, the sufficiency of the driving forces is explored. If there is a lack of motivation to make sustained change, then that deficiency has to be addressed. Next, the behaviors that form barriers to goal achievement are explored for significance and amelioration. Research suggests that working to overcome and eradicate the restraining forces is much more efficient for achieving sustained change than is continuing to push on the driving side of the equation.[33]

Placing all of that rich feedback information into a systems perspective—one that considers the driving and restraining forces in terms of a specific goal—enables decision making based on looking at the information as a whole. This is quite different from the non-reflective and all-too-familiar approach of picking the first viable option for change and, when that proves to be insufficient, searching for another possible option, and so on. By considering all of the factors at the same time, we make the type of powerful jump we achieve when we use research based on structured equation modeling (multiple variables evaluated at the same time) rather than on correlation analysis (one variable evaluated at a time). The systemic approach, looking at all the variables at once, allows for better understanding of the multiple factors at work and helps to prioritize efforts and avoid unintended consequences.

LEVEL FIVE: SUSTAINING CHANGE

Goal: Strengthen individual efforts with reinforcement from a supportive system to sustain change.

The learning I gleaned over years of work using a myriad of change models[34] is that creating a supportive system ensures the best chance of sustainability. This learning came from observing how these well-known models worked only so far in driving sustained change. One of the most widely recognized executive coaches, Marshall Goldsmith, makes expressed efforts to engage others in the coaching process, at times even including family members.[35]

A core tenant of TEC is that the goal of coaching is not to just help the executive change behavior A or B or C. The higher-level goal is to help executives master the skills to sustain the current changes and to create a feedback environment with the reflective space that lets them learn what they need in order to solve future leadership challenges. Sustained change is the culmination of a safe and trusting holding environment that enables authentic relationships to be built and facilitates expanded feedback and reflection opportunities, which in turn provide the quality information that can be contextualized by thinking in systems. The entire process is in service to making the changes that are critical to achieving stated goals.

Five elements distinguish haphazard goals from those with true commitment for results:

- The willingness to share the goal
- The commitment to measure success
- Value-anchored behavioral changes

- The engagement of a support team to provide ongoing support and feedback
- The manageability of the scale of the change

Willingness to Share the Goal

The willingness to share the goal was introduced in the relationship-building phase, the second level of the Hierarchy of Sustained Change. Sharing the goal creates the potential for trusted others to provide specific feedback. This process begins a contained experience of mutual risk taking. When an individual takes the risk of sharing targeted developmental areas, those who provide feedback respond by taking the risk of sharing insights and perspectives that might otherwise not be articulated. This approach, treating proactive development in an open and positive manner, is quite different from what sometimes happens when coaching is hidden and treated as a secret that no one should know about.

Commitment to Measure Success

The commitment to measure success is a foundational attitude or mind-set of anyone who is serious about achieving and sustaining results. The clarity and specificity of the goal generates reciprocated clarity and specificity of feedback that can be used to modify behaviors and take actions that overcome the barriers and support goal achievement.

Value-Anchored Behavioral Change

The commitment to sustain results also reveals itself in the willingness to explore the values that anchor specific behaviors. The concept is simple: values drive behavior, either consciously or subconsciously. Over time, we tend to behave congruently with our values. The corollary is that if you want to change behaviors, you need to understand the values that support behavior A and the values that would support behavior B. I ask executives to explore their internal value system to assure alignment with the new behaviors and to build motivation for making the targeted changes. This concept is quite different from the adage that all we need to drive change is more willpower.

One executive shared her frustration at receiving low marks for not being sufficiently "warm and fuzzy." She elaborated how she tried to compensate for this perception by engaging in empathic listening, even when she did not have the time or empathy. She felt her efforts resulted in giving out lots of "atta boys" for behaviors she considered basic. Imagine her frustration after engaging in these contrived behaviors and still hearing that it was not enough. Yet when we talked, the values that really mattered to her immediately surfaced. She had a rich pool of high-potency values, such as a passion for excellence and a commitment to professional success coupled with personal satisfaction. She felt pressured to give praise when she did not feel it was earned and was fearful of directly saying so because of how she would be branded. As a result, the praise she gave came across as forced or even disingenuous. As Arnold Beisser wrote in an article on the paradox of change, "Change occurs when one becomes what he is, not when he tries to become what he is not."[36]

Engagement of a Support Team

The fourth element of sustained change is the engagement of a support team. Powerful models of change, those involving intractable situations and high-stake results, come from the health field.[37] Alcoholics Anonymous' twelve-step program is built around a strong support group, as is the Weight Watchers program. Investments in each level of this model culminate in the development of an active and engaged support group that can provide ongoing feedback.

Manageability of the Scale of Change

The fifth element of sustained change is the scale of the change. We work in groups, on cross-functional teams, and in organizations. While working at Scientific Methods, Dr. Robert Blake, who co-developed the Managerial Grid and headed the company, shared his frustration at the way people would be changed by his intense week-long workshops only to revert to old behaviors under the weight of returning to their corporate culture. His model of change was critically anchored to the culture of the corporation. By design, the Hierarchy of Sustained Change model is built on one-on-one relationships. The potency of the model is that it can be realized without a dependency on massive organization-wide change.

DEVELOPING THE TRANSFORMATIONAL EXECUTIVE COACHING MODEL

The Hierarchy of Sustained Change detailed above provides the grounding for the Seven-Stage Model. The model has been refined over years based on feedback from clients, reflections on what worked and what did not work, post-engagement discussions on what was still working, and an overarching commitment to the development of a transformational model of coaching that helps organizations gain efficiencies through the development of their executives and helps executives become better leaders and people.

The model of coaching described in Chapter 3 has been evolving over the past two decades, and it will continue to evolve based on insights and feedback offered by executives who willingly put themselves on the line to raise the bar for their leadership.

It started, as many traditional models of coaching do, with building blocks for gathering inputs, developing goals, crafting an action plan, and measuring for success.[38] As an example of how this model has evolved, it was a challenging coaching engagement that led to the basic structure of the model. In an earlier phase in my coaching career, when I was regularly using standard 360-degree feedback assessments, I met with an executive who absorbed the positive and "pushed back" on the first development item he heard. He insisted that the less-than-positive feedback scores were just not right and he countered with stories about his successes. His tone was defensive, masked behind bravado. While holding the possibility that he was right, I was also mindful of how leaders frequently inflate self-ratings and the consequential risks of career derailment.[39]

Rather than disagreeing with him and risking a power struggle, I was able to move past his right-wrong framing by shifting his focus to one of curiosity about how his staff perceived him on goals that he cared about. We ended this reflective conversation with a collaborative commitment to develop the goals he wanted to master. I adapted a tool that I had been using with other clients, converting it into an interview protocol built around his goals and the behaviors that either supported or undermined achieving those goals. The results were so impactful that this methodology for gathering valid and usable data has become a core structure of the Seven-Stage Model.

The goal-results focus taps into my pragmatic business side, fostered by years of both managerial and executive-level responsibilities. Leaders who expect to get results do better with clearly articulated goals. The old wag, "If you don't know where you are going, any direction is as good as another" comes to mind. Using an assessment process that is highly attuned to the client's goals gets the client invested in the learning process.[40]

Prior to creating the interview protocol, I had been using this systems approach of exploring the driving and restraining forces to change with my coaching clients. Initially, I was surprised at the excited reaction they had to more deeply understanding the systems in which they operated. The elegant force field tool provided an easily accessible way of exploring whether the issues were around not enough driving forces (rarely the case) or the restraining forces (often the culprit, but typically poorly articulated). The actions to overcome the restraining forces became the foundation for the Seven-Stage Roadmap, the action plan used to achieve sustained changes in behavior that will be introduced in Chapter 3.

Experiential learning informs this model for coaching and feedback. While research and theories support the Seven-Stage Model, the feedback from my clients has breathed life into it. My clients' insightful comments helped shape this model. It was their amazement at how colleagues responded when they put their goals out there for everyone's comments. It was having my tough-skinned executive clients' comments on the care and conscientiousness of the feedback that the participants offered them. It was the clients who felt that because of the feedback, they finally could make sense of what was going on. It was the comment from the head honcho about how brave his successor-in-training was for articulating so exactly the goals he had to work on. It was the client who insisted that he set bi-weekly meetings with each of his direct reports to further build the free-flowing feedback environment this process started. It was the senior executive who was blown away by how negatively he was perceived and who had a deep passion to change his behaviors in ways that would make his team one of the best in the entire organization. Again and again, comments from executives served as a testament to the potency of this feedback process.

Chapter Three

The Seven-Stage Model for Executive Transformation

The Transformational Executive Coaching Seven-Stage Model is a unique approach to executive coaching that provides the best information and resources available to support executives in achieving the goals that enable them to impact organizational performance. At the heart of the Seven-Stage Model is the Stakeholder Feedback Interview, designed to provide experienced executives with the quality and specificity of feedback that cannot be obtained from traditional 360-degree survey instruments or from typical employee-manager-peer interactions. Customizing the feedback process to the executive's specific goals—goals tuned to the executive's needs and current organizational circumstances—provides an entirely different level of value to the executive and the organization.

The Seven-Stage Model is designed to drive systemic and sustainable changes to behaviors that transcend the relatively short time that the executive and coach work together, mitigating the dependence of the executive on the coach. In addition to providing the initial high-quality feedback, the model impacts the organization by teaching the executive techniques for seeking feedback, which in turn enriches the feedback environment and increases the work group's effectiveness.[1] When executives have firsthand experiential knowledge of the power of goal-specific feedback that is behaviorally anchored and offered with the best intentions, they want to continue this practice. A high percentage of the executives I work with continue to use some variation of the feedback process they learned during the coaching engagement. In the best cases, the executive's use of the techniques for getting valid and usable feedback cascades into the culture of the work group and beyond. The aspirational goal behind the Seven-Stage Model is that the potency of having an enhanced feedback environment will permeate the entire organization.

The care and attention given to helping the executive learn the techniques for getting high-quality feedback reflects my philosophy of coaching, one designed into the Seven-Stage Model. Coaching provides ongoing value by expanding the executive's leadership toolkit. The tools and techniques used to master a specific issue or achieve a specific goal are discussed and generalized so that the executive can apply them in other situations. Creating transferable knowledge enables the executive to apply processes and concepts in other contexts so that the benefits of coaching transcend the current engagement.

This chapter provides an overview of the model's seven stages. Chapter 4 provides detailed descriptions of the process steps in each stage. Chapter 5 and 6 unpack coaching skills for building relationships and

TRANSFORMATIONAL EXECUTIVE COACHING SEVEN-STAGE MODEL

STAGE	DESCRIPTION AND DELIVERABLE
1. Establish Relationship	Meet the executive, review the coaching process, and determine the mutual benefit of entering into a coaching contract. Clarify what it means to work in a safe, bounded, goal-directed relationship.
2. Frame Change Intent	Guide the executive in creating an explicit statement of three or four goals that have the full support of the executive's sponsor.
3. Engage Feedback Support Team	Conduct the Stakeholder Feedback Interviews. Review the goal-directed feedback report with the executive.
4. Commit to Action	Complete the Commit to Action Worksheet that includes: (1) the key areas for behavioral development, (2) specific actions to create change, (3) an action learning project, and (4) an action plan.
5. Measure Success	At approximately five months into a six-month coaching engagement, the executive asks the same feedback support team to reevaluate the driving and restraining forces to his goals.
6. Sustain Progress	Meet with the executive and the executive's sponsor to provide a high-level overview of progress and to build ongoing support from the sponsor.
7. Provide Feedback to Coach	The executive evaluates the coach against goals that were important to the coach.

sustaining change that are needed to successfully implement the model. Chapter 7, new to this edition, addresses how coaches can get the support and reflection they need for continued growth. Chapter 8, also new to this edition, provides a model with case examples for addressing the many ethical challenges and dilemmas coaches experience.

STAGE ONE: ESTABLISH RELATIONSHIP

Meet the executive, review the coaching process, and determine the mutual benefit of entering into a coaching contract. Clarify what it means to work in a safe, bounded, goal-directed relationship.

Description

The purpose of the first stage of the Seven-Stage Model is to meet the executive, review the process, and determine the mutual desirability of entering into a coaching contract. This is often the first time the executive has had a coach, which can translate into a lot of uncertainty about the process of coaching, how issues of confidentiality are handled, and generally what to expect. These issues need to be fully addressed in ways that provide a sense of safety and confidence in both the process and the coach. In cases where the executive has received prior coaching, this first stage is needed to demonstrate how this approach differs from the model the executive was exposed to in prior coaching. This is particularly helpful when the executive's prior coaching was not effective.

Deliverable

The tangible outcome for this stage of the coaching process is a signed contract, detailing the scope of work with key deliverables, the processes to be employed, the meeting and communication logistics, and how success will be measured.

The intangible outcome for this stage of the coaching process is the executive feeling comfortable with a coaching model built on attunement, authenticity, and collaboration and feeling safe to discuss the real issues. Building safety requires a healthy conversation about how the coach handles confidentiality. The executive should know that only he will get copies of the feedback reports and that the coach will respond to questions about progress from the sponsor or human resources by discussing only process and inviting the executive to share content. Sharing detailed examples of how I handled "invitations" to violate confidentiality has been reassuring to clients.

As with all issues of trust, this process may take time. One executive took several sessions to be convinced that the conversations were confidential. He signaled this uncertainty with reminders such as, "I would not be having these conversations if it were not for the confidentiality." That was an opportunity for me to reinforce how I manage boundaries. I shared snippets from conversations I had with his vice president of human resources, including how normal it was for the person in that position to ask certain questions and how I routinely responded. Trust increases when it has been tested.

The confidentiality boundary management is particularly significant when coaching multiple clients within the same organization. In several organizations, I individually coached the members of the executive team. This model of coaching has been exceptionally effective, as it enables the coach to add the value of seeing the entire system, with insight into issues from the political, cultural, human resources, and structural perspectives. It also mandates having an earned reputation for not sharing information between clients.

My approach to coaching actually starts during the initial

interview, where the executive and the coach explore whether they have the right chemistry and the desire to work together. While I use this initial meeting to explore the executive's purpose for seeking a coach, I also use it to demonstrate my approach to coaching through my behaviors.

Understanding the executive's motivations for entering into a coaching contract is critical to the selection process. When I first began my coaching work, I assumed that the client's motivation was always high. More than two decades later, I now start with an open perspective, aware that I do not know the client's level of motivation and thus need to gain that insight from the interview. In the small number of cases where I sense the motivation is not high, I talk about the difficulties clients can have with making and sustaining behavioral changes. This invites a conversation on how much change they are considering and how dedicated they are to the task of changing behaviors.

Low motivation can show itself as low commitment. A conversation on the commitment to change was necessary with a mid-level regional executive who insisted at our first meeting that he just wanted to "make a few adjustments, nothing serious." I pushed back on that to determine both how sure he was about that being the case and how invested he was in making the commitment to the coaching process. I suggested that before we move forward, we consider how much investment is required—his time, my time, his boss's time, and the time of those who will be providing him feedback. I asked if the return of investment would be acceptable if we were only making a few tweaks. This directness without defensiveness or aggression on my part opened up a dialogue that uncovered his cynicism about coaching. This dialogue gave me the opportunity to showcase how I work by expressing empathetic attunement as a former executive, genuine concern for his interests, and a clear commitment to working collaboratively on his goals. This candid conversation enabled the executive to make an informed choice about whether he was willing to engage in the coaching process at this time and whether I was the coach he wanted to work with.

While the executive I've mentioned above decided to embrace coaching and had outcomes that went far beyond "a few adjustments, nothing serious," other executives self-select out of the process. I have too much respect for the hard work of coaching and the executives I work with to accept low expectations for outcomes due to low motivation or any other reason. Some of these interviews result in the selection of another coach or a deferral on starting the engagement. The "hard work of coaching" is not just about the executive or the coach; because the Seven-Stage Model is a systemic approach, it involves many people. Using this method to achieve systemic and sustainable change requires a determined effort by the executive, the coach, and the executive's support team.

When I described this process to one junior executive, she expressed her concern that this was more time, energy, and personal investment than she wanted to take on. I respected that decision and acknowledged that right now might not be the best time for her to start a six-month coaching engagement. Executives are busy people with complex roles who are always juggling demands. There are definitely times that are not conducive to this work. I realize, and make it easy for the executive to understand, that this model of coaching requires a significant commitment and also raises the bar for results.

During a recent selection interview, the executive expressed relief upon learning that coaching was not about lowering the bar. While he knew he could be hard on his team, expected a lot, and sometimes moved at a faster pace, he also knew the solution was not to accept a lower standard of work. He twice repeated his increased comfort when he learned that my coaching model was about keeping standards high and delivering results. Our open conversations enabled him to go forward and to affirm his commitment to the process and work.

STAGE TWO: FRAME CHANGE INTENT

Guide the executive in creating an explicit statement of three or four goals that have the full support of the executive's sponsor.

Description

With the coaching contract and the foundations for a working relationship established, the first few meetings detail the preliminary goals and aspirations for the coaching engagement.

Deliverable

The deliverable for this phase of coaching is a written statement of three or four explicit goals that have the full support of both the executive and the executive's sponsor.

When working with seasoned executives, I find that through conversation we can adequately identify the areas worthy of our attention. Seasoned executives have lengthy experience with assessments and evaluations and with bosses who have been direct about their developmental needs. The coaching process adds the reflection necessary to synthesize and make sense of the data the executive already has available. This is significantly different from coaching models that rely on gathering new data, most often through a 360-degree survey instrument, before beginning to assemble a set of goals. The 360-degree survey process is good for leaders with less tenure and a low awareness of how others perceive their strengths and weaknesses, but it undervalues the knowledge already present at the executive level. Those surveys typically provide a Likert scale rating across a broad spectrum of leadership competencies.

Developing well-articulated goals that motivate the executive flows from a process that finds the intersection of multiple frames or perspectives. The Seven-Stage Model explores goals from three perspectives: (1) business issues, (2) personal leadership challenges, and (3) the executive's career aspirations. The objective is to help executives define goals that cross all three perspectives and are in alignment with their values. Later chapters will address how this process works and will provide examples of what can happen if all three dimensions are not considered. The Venn diagram shown in Figure 2 captures this concept of goals that concurrently impact the three perspectives.

FIGURE 2: EXPLORE GOALS FROM THREE PERSPECTIVES

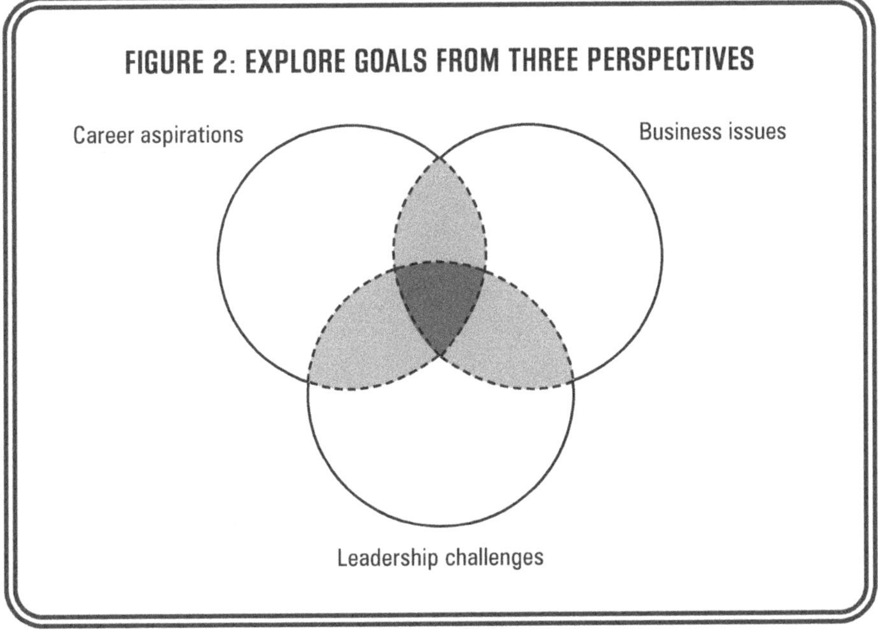

Once these few critical goals are well articulated, I meet with the executive and the sponsor to ensure that we have the right goals and to gain the sponsor's support for achieving those goals.

The sponsor most typically is the executive's boss and will sometimes be an interested board member. Before making substantive investments of time and involving a lot of other people, it is prudent to ensure managerial alignment. Two experiences illustrate the benefits of giving the sponsor the opportunity to influence the goals. In one case, the executive sponsor wanted to show his direct report that he was invested and committed, and opportunities to influence the goals gave him a way to demonstrate that. In another case, a reluctant executive sponsor got pulled into investing in the process. The more she got involved, the more committed she was to a successful outcome. Involving the sponsor also serves as a "reality check" for potential blind spots. I have seen no downside to getting the executive sponsor invested in the behavioral change process.

One of my clients was a bit hesitant to engage his boss, convinced that he would not add much value to the goal-setting process. When I asked why he held that view, he laughed and described how infrequently he received any feedback and how cursory it was. When I asked about performance reviews, he simply noted, "Those don't happen at this level." I have found that to be quite a common occurrence. Executives do not get the specific, behaviorally anchored feedback they could use to guide change.[2] When we held a three-way meeting of the executive, his boss, and me, the executive's boss got involved and had solid ideas. My client later shared that he had never expected his boss to be as engaged or animated as he was during the meeting. He was surprised at how helpful his boss was in refining and adding a long-term career-planning focus to his goals. The Seven-Stage Model undergirds the feedback process by creating the context and providing the structure so that members of the feedback support team know what is expected and how to respond.

STAGE THREE: ENGAGE FEEDBACK SUPPORT TEAM

Conduct the Stakeholdeer Feedback Interviews. Review the goal-directed feedback report with the executive.

Description

In most coaching models this phase would be referred to as the data-collection phase, with a goal of getting a broad range of perspectives from many people on an array of leadership competencies. To this end, a 360-degree survey instrument is typically administered. I propose a different goal for this step and, in the tradition of Louis Sullivan and his understudy Frank Lloyd Wright's dictum "form follows function," a different process. The Seven-Stage Model drives systemic and sustainable changes to behavior, which happens with a cadre of knowledgeable and caring colleagues who are willing to forgo anonymity and share openly what the executive needs to hear in order to make meaningful changes. The Stakeholder Feedback Interview process includes defining the interview protocol, carefully selecting the participants, conducting the interviews, summarizing the themes across the various interviews, and reviewing the report with the executive.

Once the proposed feedback support team has been identified, the executive contacts the team members to get their agreement to serve in this role, explains the interview process that will be used, and electronically introduces the executive coach. The coach conducts thirty-minute telephone interviews with between six and eight people (boss, peers, and direct reports), using a variation of the Stakeholder Feedback Interview Protocol, included in this book as Appendix B.

The critical elements of the protocol are:

- Specific questions on behaviors that either support or get in the way of achieving each goal
- Qualitative, behaviorally anchored responses
- A request made at both the beginning and end of the interview to share the notes taken during the phone conversation

Participation on this support team carries a reciprocal obligation. The expansion of the feedback environment starts by having the executive share his goals, the things that are most important to him to work on, with people that he trusts, those who know him in the work context and who he believes have his best interests at heart.

The screening criteria for entrance onto the feedback support team are:

- The executive's confidence that the participant has his best interests at heart
- The participant's contemporary knowledge of the executive's behaviors relative to the specific goals
- The participant's willingness to share insights on the executive's specific goals

Deliverable

The deliverable for the Stakeholder Feedback Interviews is a substantive report of highly organized feedback of both behaviors that support goal achievement (driving forces) and behaviors that undermine goal achievement (restraining forces.) The synthesized report identifies themes, while the individual interview reports (one from each interview) provide support detail.

I had a client who received some major changes to his goals from his boss. Then his boss went further and suggested that four specific people be added to the pool of individuals being considered for inclusion on the feedback support team. My client and I had already reviewed the criteria and had a proposed list, and we knew that one of those four did not meet the criteria. This created a feedback opportunity. I was able to describe the criteria for inclusion and asked my client to share why he disqualified one individual. The boss listened intently, gave clear indications that he understood, and supported the executive's proposed list.

Executives do not talk about making themselves vulnerable, yet that is exactly what happens when they ask for the feedback that really matters on the goals that are most important to them. I still remember one executive who realized how vulnerable this process made him feel and, in classic form, leaned back in his chair, put his hands behind his head, and deeply exhaled before taking the step of becoming vulnerable. He needed assurance that his direct reports would not take advantage of his being open about his goals. After the feedback process, he was overwhelmed by how gracious the members of his executive team were, how they willingly reciprocated his trust and openly shared explicit information with examples of behaviors they had observed firsthand.

Building trust happens as we take risks. The executive is taking the risk of sharing the areas targeted for development. The authenticity of the goals should be abundantly clear to the members of the feedback support team and should set the stage for reciprocation at that same level of authenticity in their interview responses. One executive, head of a large global operation, had been diligent in developing his goals. He approached them with the same sharpness of attention that he applied to his multi-thousand-person operation. The goals included a business outcome, a statement of what he wanted to build on, and a constraining force to be balanced. For example, in order to increase profits, he had to continue to build the organization in a specific area while recognizing his tendency to get too far ahead without informing his executive committee. His boss and others blew this executive away by praising him for taking the courage to so clearly articulate the issues. The executive was admitting exactly where he had to improve.

STAGE FOUR: COMMIT TO ACTION

Complete the Commit to Action Worksheet that includes (1) the key areas for behavioral development, (2) specific actions to create change, (3) an action learning project, and (4) an action plan.

Description

The feedback process generates balanced feedback on both the things that help and the things that get in the way. We review the driving forces to see if these are sufficient, to see if there are additional things that the executive should be doing to achieve the goal. Things that get in the way of the executives accomplishing their goals are the restraining forces. Kurt Lewin, a seminal thinker in applying systems concepts to behavioral science, argued that we should pay most attention to the restraining forces, the things that are getting in the way.[3] We explore the restraining forces to identify which ones to address and eradicate.

One of the powerful benefits of using a systems approach is that it avoids the pitfall of framing things as either strengths or weaknesses. In this model, a behavior may be a potential driving force for one goal and a potential restraining force for another goal. An example is the nearly universal executive tendency to be "impatient for results." For some goals that tendency definitely provides the needed drive to completion, while for other goals it overruns the benefit of more circumspect decision making. The historical management approach of focusing primarily on aspects labeled as weaknesses or career derailers has led to a backlash trend of techniques that focus primarily or solely on the positive.[4] This post-modern positive approach has been found wanting by some critics because it lacks a systemic perspective. In the TEC model, both sides of the force field matter as they relate to the specific goals the executive has targeted.

This stage requires a significant investment of time for the executive to metabolize the feedback and to isolate the few critical areas to work on. The potency of using a behaviorally anchored process[5] to gather the feedback on the executive's goals becomes apparent at this step, where the executive makes commitments to changes in behavior.

Deliverable

Once feedback has been analyzed and reviewed, the coaching engagement moves on to the action plan or Seven-Stage Roadmap (see Appendix A).

This stage includes four critical components:

- Identification of key areas for behavioral development
- Commitment to take specific actions
- Selection of a real, on-the-job action learning project
- Development of a metricized action plan

This detailed roadmap becomes a work in progress that guides the coaching conversations and serves to hold the executive accountable for her commitments.

Identification of Key Areas

I coached an executive who recognized that he was not viewed as being inclusive of all members of his executive team; consequently, he crafted a goal targeting his desire to create a culture marked with high levels of diversity and inclusion. The interview process to gather behavioral data powerfully captured a barrier to achieving this goal. One of the few female members of his executive committee noted how frequently meetings at that time of year began with conversations about hunting trips over the weekend. She went on to describe how this left her feeling alienated from the group and somewhat disgusted by the gory details. This well-articulated example of a specific behavior and impact did several things. First, my client understood how this senior vice president felt excluded. Second, and more important, it opened our conversation about the role that "coming together as a group" plays in setting a tone of inclusion and about techniques for testing for inclusion in a group. The commitment plan had actions that ensured inclusion. The executive made sharing outside activities an intentional part of the meeting as a way to build inclusion and attune all members of the executive committee. In this new context, hunting stories were still shared, albeit without the field-dressing descriptions.

Commitment to take Specific Actions

The second component, the commitment to take specific actions, is crucial to gaining sustained change. I use the disciplines developed in the action-learning research to ensure that the executive pinpoints practical, tangible opportunities to practice the new, desired behaviors.[6] At its heart, action learning is a process for working on real problems, taking action, and learning through reflective questioning and listening while solving the targeted challenge.

One executive targeted a variation on the goal of being more effective at leading teams. We narrowed our coaching efforts to one specific team he was leading that included executives from more than a dozen different countries and developed a toolkit of techniques he planned to use and actions he planned to take at the meetings. He recruited two trusted team members who were also participants in his feedback process to share with him how he executed his goals during the meetings. Our coaching conversations became a continual learning and refining process, building on what worked and adapting to changing situations. The eventual results stunned the client, the trusted participants, and the executive's sponsor. People went from dreading being on a team with this "tyrant" to recruiting him for team leadership positions. On one of the executive's international projects, the company credited his leadership skills with aligning stakeholders and inspiring a team in efforts that accelerated the timetable and resulted in a savings of many millions of dollars.

Selection of an Action Learning Project

The Center for Creative Leadership, one of the most respected leadership development organizations, builds its programs on an assessment-challenge-support model, recognizing the importance of having the opportunity to practice new behaviors in a supportive environment with professional guidance/coaching and with fast feedback loops.[7] In my role as a consultant, I have formally evaluated the effectiveness of leadership development programs. I did this for a well-respected state-level organization, using the success-case research methodology developed by Brinkerhoff.[8] When I compared senior managers who had clear and measurable success against those with performance metrics at the other end of the bell curve, one of the explanatory variables was whether they had a work context for applying what they learned in their leadership development program.

When I reviewed my own successes as a coach, I found the same variable surfacing as making a difference. Executives who selected a bounded, targeted area to practice the new behaviors have better results. This makes intuitive sense: it forces the executive to move from concept to practice in a select area, it supports motivation with early wins, it provides immediate feedback on what is working, it provides fast adaption and modification support, and it bounds the time frame for making the changes. It also helps that the coaching work is now the "real work" of the business, not something "extra."

Development of a Metricized Action Plan

Measuring results is often treated as an afterthought in coaching. With my finance background and work in metrics for soft skill development, I take another perspective; of course, we should be able to capture and recognize changes in behavior. One executive, a transplant from the semiconductor industry, was reluctant to enter into a coaching engagement where there were no clear indicators of progress. He was excited by being able to demonstrate results. To me, the proof of his commitment was in how carefully he sized and time-lined what he expected to accomplish. He saw the process of establishing metrics as invigorating and as a positive challenge. His goal focus and drive kicked in as a self-fulfilling prophecy. While measuring success is the fifth stage of the Seven-Stage Model, establishing that results will be measured and agreeing on the process for gathering that data is part of the Commit to Action stage.

STAGE FIVE: MEASURE SUCCESS

At approximately five months into a six-month coaching engagement, the executive asks the same feedback support team to reevaluate the driving and restraining forces to his goals.

Description

This stage of the coaching engagement consists of teaching the executive how to gather ongoing data relevant to goal achievement. We can expect to see sustained behavioral changes in a six-month coaching engagement. At the same time, it is generally an insufficient period of time in which to see differences in the bottom line, revenues, or other multi-determined outcome metrics.

Deliverable

The Seven-Stage Model design wonderfully supports the ability to measure outcomes. The executive has identified crisp goals and has a wealth of data on the behaviors that support goal achievement and undermine goal achievement. At approximately five months into the six-month coaching engagement, I invite the client to ask the same feedback support team to reevaluate the driving and restraining forces that are operating on the goals. Such feedback provides a pre-coaching/post-coaching comparison.

I had a coaching engagement that was nine months rather than six because it required work with the team as a whole, and the executive had been working on significant changes that involved others. Once the executive started implementing the action plan, the executive management team gave him anecdotal feedback that they liked what they were seeing. I asked him to gather feedback using a more structured approach, the same one I used at the beginning of our engagement. He agreed but was nervous, not quite sure he could do what I had done. The truth is that at the beginning of the process, he could not have, because he did not have the trust and engagement of his team at that time. I knew he could at this point because of the enhanced relationships and because of the simplicity of the process. The tricky part is keeping people on task and using behaviorally anchored inputs. It's amazing how many times people get excited and want to cover everything. I use a prepared interview protocol to ensure that I manage both of these challenges (see Appendix B: Stakeholder Feedback Interview Protocol). I reviewed the process with my client and suggested he observe while I interviewed one of his direct reports. I had ample opportunities to shape the inputs; for example, "While it is great you think John Doe is doing better, what would you point to as an example of something he did that led you to that conclusion?" My client watched quietly and then conducted the next interview with another direct report while I observed. After a short debrief and a few insights, he independently held conversations with the rest of his executive management team. The results provided a dramatically different story than the first set of interviews. The team was able to save $4 million in the next budget cycle through better collaboration, and the executive management team genuinely felt they had put the fun back into their work.

After the client gathers the feedback, we compare the new post-coaching results to those gathered at the beginning of the process and discuss surprises and learnings. We review the pre-coaching and post-coaching results, with an eye to (1) supporting and reinforcing improvements in order to minimize backsliding, and (2) looking for areas that have stubbornly resisted movement and determining what else needs to be done. For most executives, the celebration for successes might last five minutes, followed by a tight focus on the next goals. The pushback from my side is to stay ever vigilant, to avoid the siren call of new goals before habitualizing the new behaviors and to ensure that when our coaching engagement ends, the gains will not dissipate.

STAGE SIX: SUSTAIN PROGRESS

Meet with the executive and the executive's sponsor to provide a high-level overview of progress and to build ongoing support from the sponsor.

Description

Reviewing the feedback gained before and after the work of coaching helps the executive metabolize the extent of the changes she has made. It also opens the door for a conversation on barriers to sustainability. Our conversations center on how the executive would know if she were backsliding. If this were a weight-loss program, it would be easy: you get on a scale at the same time every day. There is an equivalent for making behavioral change, and our work is to articulate how we stay alert to any backsliding. This stage is about surfacing and addressing those realities.

Deliverable

One technique to ensure continuity and sustainability of success is a closure conversation with the executive and the sponsor. This meeting provides a high-level overview of progress made and builds in ongoing support from the sponsor. The executive has the opportunity to share facets of the pre-coaching and post-coaching feedback that has been gathered.

In a memorable coaching engagement, I decided I could skip this closure meeting, as the executive's sponsor was not particularly engaged in the process and the executive was very independent. This was a mistake. The sponsor felt dropped and expressed concern that the executive being coached had just done his duty of getting coached and had "checked the box." The sponsor viewed herself as a mentor and wanted to continue to be engaged, and she had leading-edge issues to convey. I learned all this about three weeks after I thought the engagement was finished. The silver lining is that I received the feedback that I needed to hear and was able to take action to gain closure through a three-way meeting. The Seven-Stage Model embeds a process that gets people involved in supporting the executive's development. Executive sponsors like that and generally want to continue to be involved, which helps ensure sustainability and continuity after the coach exits the process.

An executive who was surprised by the feedback he received and felt misunderstood demonstrated an exemplary method of sustaining progress. Because the feedback was so explicit and because people were willing to own their perspective by sharing their names, he was able to start regular conversations, and structured bimonthly meetings with various people to help keep him on track. By the end of the coaching engagement, I felt he had already supplanted me with a trusted feedback support team and regularly scheduled conversations. Perfect!

STAGE SEVEN: PROVIDE FEEDBACK TO COACH

The executive evaluates the coach against goals that were important to the coach.

Description

At the end of the engagement, I always ask the executives to evaluate me, the coach, using an evidence-based methodology. This is in the spirit of "eating your own cooking." I structure the feedback into five domains. The first is on preconditions that enable success—motivation, chemistry, and opportunity to apply learnings. The second domain is the things I should be doing as a coach, the standards to which I hold myself accountable. The third domain is on outcomes, the things that our coaching engagement was expected to deliver. In the fourth domain, I ask for any "ah-ha moments," those points in the process when the executive really got something that would make a lasting difference. Finally, I explore return-on-investment metrics.

Deliverable

The feedback report on the coach is completed in both an online and a face-to-face format. The form used (see Appendix D: Evidence-Based Coaching Evaluation) is provided in advance to the executive. Some prefer to complete it in advance while others prefer to complete it through conversation.

This feedback has refined and even transformed how I coach. Coaches ask clients to engage a support team for feedback because research has made clear that self-assessment ratings are not accurate. It makes perfect sense that this self-rating deficiency would apply to the coach as well.

I use these reports to look for patterns and to hold myself to the same standard as my client. Why did these particular cases yield such outstanding executive reviews? What did I do differently that led to the higher levels of perceived trust? How did the use of the action learning project impact the results? An example of a refinement that resulted from feedback is the additional attention I now give to building relationship as the first step. An example of a transformational change is converting from traditional 360-degree survey instruments with anonymous raters, averaged scores, and online technology to the Stakeholder Feedback Interview methodology.

As an executive coach, my clients expect me to hold them accountable for meeting their commitments, whether that is honoring their appointments or working on their action learning projects. Sometimes it is tempting to let the missed commitments pass without comment. I did this with one executive, and at the end of the six-month engagement he rated me low on holding him accountable. When I asked for the specifics, he quickly and accurately related how I assigned tasks for him to do between sessions and did not follow up on those, waiting for him to bring them up. He explained how this caused him to question my commitment to his success. Ouch!

During the next year, I had the opposite experience. I began taking notes on assignments and listing those as agenda items at the beginning of the next session. Another executive shared how much he appreciated the accountability. It aligned with how he wanted to lead, and more important to me, it opened conversations on what was getting in the way whenever a commitment started to slide.

The acceptance of feedback as a normal and highly valuable source of rich information comes from my early business career, my academic work, and my ongoing coaching work. I have the privilege to serve as an adjunct professor, teaching graduate students topics on leadership and ethics, at St. Edward's University. This small liberal arts college places a premium on student feedback. Our program director was blunt, "Bad reviews, and I will fire you." This was not bravado for adjunct professors; he did just that to several teachers I thought were solid. My first few semesters, I waited with bated breath for the student evaluations to come in, and then I developed a different attitude to the feedback. I started to proactively seek it, to get the students' input on curriculum changes I planned. I was impressed with how seriously they took this opportunity. For example, when I asked if I should cut back on the outside reading, easing their study load, I was told flat out, "No, that is just too important." Seeking feedback in a deliberate, structured, and constructive way is our best path to growing and learning.

The Seven-Stage Model follows process stages, uses a unique Stakeholder Feedback Interview methodology, and creates a feedback support team to drive systemic and sustainable changes to behaviors that transcend the relatively short time that the executive and coach work together.

Chapter Four

Coaching Through the Transformational Process

The previous chapter describes the Seven-Stage Model as a unique approach to executive coaching, one that gets executives the best information and resources available to support them in achieving their goals that enable them to impact organizational performance. In this chapter, the processes used to achieve those results are detailed. A significant portion of this chapter will describe the Stakeholder Feedback Interview process, the data-collection stage of the model, which is at the heart of how the executives get the high-quality information. Some traditional 360-degree instruments offer the option of customizing the survey by adding open-ended questions, which certainly improves the quality of feedback data collected. The Seven-Stage Model takes customization much further by tailoring the entire survey to the executive's unique needs. The resulting report derives its potency from the fact that all of the feedback is provided in response to goal-focused questions.

It is rewarding to guide leaders through these process steps and help them learn techniques that create an expanded feedback environment. This chapter describes the process steps in each of the stages of the model and how they fit together to create the desired results.

STAGE ONE: ESTABLISH RELATIONSHIP

STAGE ONE: ESTABLISH RELATIONSHIP	
PROCESS STEP	**DESCRIPTION**
a. Set out process and relationship expectations.	Guide the interview while clarifying expectations on process, relationship, and outcomes.
b. Demonstrate coaching style.	Demonstrate coaching style and techniques by translating the business issues and leadership challenges into potential goals.
c. Follow up.	Send a short thank-you note and summarize a few areas where the work might be focused.
d. Get a signed contract.	Detail expectations and deliverables in a formal document, signed by both parties.

The first stage, Establish Relationship, consists of three processes related to defining and clarifying expectations and a final process for both the formal and informal contract.

Stage One. Process Step a.
Set out process and relationship expectations:

Guide the interview while clarifying expectations on process, relationship, and outcomes.

The first process step is to clarify expectations. The coach should take the initiative on how the meeting will proceed, as many executives have not previously worked with a coach and will be curious about what to expect. The hour-long meeting has three segments. In the first segment, the coach asks the executive to describe the business challenges she is facing and then the leadership challenges she is experiencing. It is also valuable to discover why she wants coaching at this particular time, exploring what she wants to achieve and whether there is a precipitating event.

The coach uses the second segment of the meeting to provide his own background, and to link his experiences and the coaching process to the executive's situation. The coach pays particular attention to building a safe, confidential environment where issues can be fully aired. An overview of the coaching process and outcome expectations, with sufficient time for questions, builds confidence in the value of starting a coaching engagement. A further connection is built through conversation about the stages of the model, the unique Stakeholder Feedback Interview method for collecting data, and the logistics for meeting.

Over time, I have become more deliberate in describing the stages of the model and how each has its own deliverable and builds on what comes before. This gives the prospective client an opportunity to ask questions and become comfortable with me and the process. One client shared how my following a formal process gave her confidence that this "whole coaching thing" would be successful.

When done well, the coach has described the process expectations and has modeled how he builds the coaching relationship. When done well, the executive feels safety and trust in the coaching relationship and confident in both the coach and the coach's process.

Stage One. Process Step b. Demonstrate coaching style:

Demonstrate coaching style and techniques by translating the business issues and leadership challenges into potential goals.

The third segment of the interview is used to begin the work of coaching. This is done by helping the executive move from business and leadership challenges to potential goals. As the executive describes the business and leadership challenges she faces, the coach is forming hypotheses and questions about how these will be shaped into goals. These hypotheses are tested during the conversation. The coach uses the same techniques and style as he would with an executive who is already being coached, which is the point. The executive can make a selection decision based on how the coach actually works. Chapter 6 describes the typical coaching skills employed in this step, including the ability to empathetically connect with the executive's situation and reframe issues within a broader systems perspective. This focus on coaching skills related to the model assumes that coaches are familiar with the core competencies promulgated by the International Coaching Federation.[1] The Seven-Stage Model advocates taking the risk of giving the executive enough information to make an informed choice about whether the coach is the right person to help her successfully identify and master the challenges she faces.

One executive's boss told her that she needed to be a better leadership role model for less-tenured managers. When I pointed out the low energy her voice and body posture revealed when she relayed this, it opened a door to a conversation about how that was not something she perceived to be highly valuable. The conversation then tapped into her energy for talking about the goals that were meaningful to her. What moved another client from mundane and uninspiring goals to something that really mattered was asking him how much his career would benefit from learning how to manage tough personnel issues masterfully.

Stage One. Process Step c.
Follow up:

Send a short thank-you note and summarize a few areas where the work might be focused.

This portion of the process demonstrates the same courtesy and active engagement a candidate shows after a job interview. This is an opportunity to rejoin on something memorable in the conversation. It also gives the coach an opportunity to help the executive move from seeing problems to seeing potential goals, ones worthy of working on and achieving.

For one executive, this follow-up note gave me the opportunity to revisit areas where we discovered we had similarities and to outline several of the possible goals that surfaced during the conversation. He later shared that seeing in writing how our short conversation brought genuine issues to the surface and provided ideas for taking action gave him confidence that entering a coaching engagement was the right thing to do at this time. Seeing things in writing makes a difference.

Stage One. Process Step d.
Get a signed contract:

Detail expectations and deliverables in a formal document, signed by both parties.

The effort that goes into a coaching contract reflects how foundational it is to the success of the coaching engagement. While there has to be a formalized contract that is typically signed by human resources and that is used to guide fee payment, I use an abbreviated version of this document, one without fee structures, to highlight the stages of coaching and the expected deliverables.

STAGE TWO: FRAME CHANGE INTENT

STAGE TWO: FRAME CHANGE INTENT	
PROCESS STEP	**DESCRIPTION**
a. Seek concurrent goals.	Seek goals that concurrently address business issues, leadership challenges, and career aspirations.
b. Narrow the goals.	Explore the issues that are most important to the executive and identify the three or four most important developmental goals.
c. Affirm executive sponsor support.	Conduct a three-way meeting (executive, coach, and executive sponsor) to test the goals for organizational alignment and sponsor support.
d. Formalize the goals.	Begin building this portion of the Seven-Stage Roadmap by documenting the written goals that have been agreed upon.

The second stage is framing the intention to change by honing in on the executive's critical goals. This stage typically takes two or three sessions to complete. Tightly focused goals enhance the quality and relevance of the behavioral insights gained during the Stakeholder Feedback Interview process. Setting challenging and yet achievable goals is as much an art as a science. There are four core processes within this second stage that move the executive from thinking expansively to narrowing choices to gaining sponsorship support to making written commitments.

Stage Two. Process Step a.
Seek concurrent goals:

Seek goals that concurrently address business issues, leadership challenges, and career aspirations.

Executives are invited to consider their goals from each of three frames or perspectives, one at a time (see diagram in Figure 2 on page 45):

- Business issues
- Personal leadership challenges
- The executive's career aspirations

The use of multiple lenses in setting goals has proven invaluable because the complexity of the executive's job typically requires balancing priorities. Starting with the business issues context ensures that the coaching is aligned with the company's preeminent concerns. Understanding how those issues amplify the leadership challenges faced by the executive further ensures an orientation on the things that matter most. A vital discussion centers on what the executive needs in order to be successful in his role. Finally, attending to the career aspirations of the executive ensures that the work is highly motivating. Chapter 6 reviews the art of finding the right balance with goals that concurrently touch on all three areas and includes techniques for addressing issues; examples range from an executive who was enthusiastic about setting goals that covered all three domains but was not sure how to do that, to the executive who was adamant that tending to his own career aspirations should not be a factor, not even a distant third.

Stage Two. Process Step b. Narrow the goals:

Explore the issues that are most important to the executive and identify the three or four most important developmental goals.

The next part of the process is to narrow those multi-perspective goals into the critical few that the executive is willing to commit to achieve or to make substantial progress on within the time frame of the coaching engagement. Asking the executive to articulate his criteria for including or excluding a goal helps uncover his operational values and beliefs. This clarity taps into the executive's authenticity around what is important. Understanding how goals are aligned with underlying values provides motivation. People have more energy for change that supports how they want to show up in the world as opposed to what they perceive as an external requirement. Additionally, being explicit about values creates a personal "brand" and makes it easier for others to understand the executive's motivation and thus his behavior. Leadership research and such notable authors as Jim Kouzes and Warren Bennis identify communicating what one stands for as a leader as a major developmental hurdle.[2]

One client had a goal of promoting open and effective communication in order to ensure alignment and drive results.

The values and beliefs behind that goal were:

- His desire to be more inclusive
- His belief that diversity really does produce the best thinking
- His conviction that better information leads to better decisions
- His belief that leaders should build a tolerance for hearing differences

Some goals are well suited for seeking feedback from a support team, and others are not. For example, one executive had a goal of building a better working relationship with a specific person with whom trust had been damaged. While that goal was addressed in the coaching engagement, it was simply excluded from the interview protocol.

The bulk of the goals will be discussed with the executive's boss, and a number of people invited to provide feedback. Therefore, even though there are career aspiration components, the goals are written with a focus on the leadership development components and the business impact.

The goal statements that are received best by these stakeholders include:

- A targeted behavioral change
- A balancing constraint or competing goal, when there is one
- A high-level outcome objective

The targeted behavioral change is placed at the forefront, as that is the statement that stays with people. The feedback participants will be more at ease providing behavioral examples when they have some sense of what is motivating the executive to change. One of the worksheets I use to ensure that executives have goals that are worthy of their time investment focuses on three attributes of the goal: outcomes, value of achieving, and possible barriers. (See Stage 2: Change Intent Worksheet in Appendix A.)

The following scenarios illustrate well-crafted goal statements.

Scenario One: Driving Productivity

Implement change at a measured pace (*behavioral change*), one that maximizes results (outcome objective) by balancing the need for increased productivity with the need to develop and retain staff (balancing constraints).

This executive was widely known for driving productivity so hard that key members of his team were burning out. The consequences were apparent in turnover, low morale, and concern that productivity enhancements were falling off target. The new thinking was to recognize the value of concurrently developing and retaining staff. The new behavior set was to be more deliberate and thoughtful about how much change the organization could handle. The coaching work was to increase the executive's skills at recognizing and addressing the human constraints to change without losing the focus on productivity.

Scenario Two: Leadership Style

Appropriately adapt my leadership style to allow for members' individual differences (behavioral change) while maintaining a high level of accountability (competing goal) in order to enhance the productivity of my teams (outcome objective).

In this example, the executive recognized that her style of leadership was not working for several members of her team, specifically in the area of delegation and follow-up activities. The competing goal served as a balancing constraint. She was willing to provide greater autonomy and range of actions, such as replacing behaviors that look like micromanaging with behaviors built on trust, as long as there was accountability for the deliverables. The challenge was how to start this process and reward early wins. We joked about the famous quote from President Ronald Reagan in his dealings with Mikhail Gorbachev, "Trust but verify." We started with that Cold War imagery and moved to deepen the levels of mutual trust.

Scenario Three: Silo Mentality

Build the executive leadership team's motivation to routinely operate with high levels of cross-departmental cooperation (behavioral change), despite an embedded silo culture (balancing constraint), in order to achieve key business metrics (outcome objective).

This newly assigned executive quickly learned that the silo mentality was undermining organizational collaboration and the achievement of several key metrics. While everyone supported the concept of collaboration, all the rewards aligned with a silo culture. From a systems perspective, this was the classic case of rewarding A while hoping for B. Exhorting the executive team to display more collaborative behaviors without addressing the factors that perpetuated the existing culture would not have led to sustained change.

Scenario Four: Just-in-Time Feedback

> Provide just-in-time feedback (behavioral change) in ways that are supportive and resolve performance issues (outcome objective).
>
> This executive's motivations were high, as her goal embraced addressing the tough issues at the right time and level and resolving those issues in ways that maintained respect and built self-accountability. She further detailed the desired outcomes goals of driving continual improvement and collaboration by adding specificity around impact on performance gaps and productivity as well as improvements to teamwork, attitudes, and habits. Finally, she spelled out several of her expected barriers with giving just-in-time feedback.

It is crucial that goals are worded in a way that is meaningful to the executive. Crafting the goals should produce some "ah-ha moments" or insights for the executive. For a client who had a passion for music, goals that linked to a conductor metaphor provided an "ah-ha moment" that seemed to give him access to the right side of his brain as he found new ways of thinking about leadership. The best goals tap into the executive's energy and drive and start the motivational juices so vital to sustaining the hard work of change.

A final check on the wording of the goals invites the executive to consider how those will be interpreted by the participants who are providing feedback. This ensures that the grammar and language is straightforward and easily understood. Occasionally, clients insist on using goal statements with complex sentence structures and compound objectives. My observation is that their feedback participants tend to get confused and some focus on only one facet of the question. The old adage about simplicity is still relevant.

There is an important distinction between the goal the client articulates and the goal as stated in the feedback interview process. While the executive is best served by identifying all three components (behavioral change, outcome objective, and balancing constraint), the support team participants are best served by focusing on the desired behavioral change. Of course, if a question comes up in the interview, the coach can provide additional context by sharing the outcome objective or balancing constraints.

The feedback support team should be impressed with the authenticity of the goals and the process. Well-articulated, on-target goals demonstrate to everyone involved that they are engaging in a meaningful process, rather than just checking off a task on a list. When the leader makes a genuine investment to improve by disclosing where he needs to develop and asks for help with learning more, that set of behaviors is greeted with a reciprocal level of investment, disclosure, and an offer of help from the other participants. This reaction from the participants in the feedback-gathering process contributes to a higher-level goal of the entire coaching engagement—building trust in the work group through a reciprocated process.

Stage Two. Process Step c.
Affirm executive sponsor support:

Conduct a three-way meeting (executive, coach, and executive sponsor) to test the goals for organizational alignment and sponsor support.

When the coach and executive are satisfied that they have arrived at the most consequential and evocative goals, the executive's boss is asked to weigh in and sign off on the goals. This step supports the process by keeping the supervisor engaged and clarifying that the goals are in organizational alignment. While on one level this step is necessary to ensure a politically correct level of information exchange, this perspective ignores the opportunity embedded in this step. Getting involvement at this stage is vital to ensuring the boss's support and engagement at later stages in the process. In highly competitive executive ranks, the impressions and views of an immediate supervisor are crucial to career success. Executives are keenly aware of the thin layer of distinction separating those who make it to the next level from those who stall out. Additionally, bosses like to influence. If there are goal components that an executive's boss thinks are critical for the organization's continued success, it is beneficial to understand that thinking and to embrace it within the developmental goal set. One client's boss was so taken with how well the executive articulated—in his words "nailed"—the real issues with the goals that he saw his direct report in a new light before the feedback process even started.

Stage Two. Process Step d.
Formalize the goals:

Begin building this portion of the Seven-Stage Roadmap by documenting the written goals that have been agreed upon.

At this process step, the coach begins to build the Seven-Stage Roadmap, which serves as the key tracking document used throughout the coaching process. The coach owns this document, tracking, editing, and updating it. (The Seven-Stage Roadmap worksheets are available in Appendix A.)

STAGE THREE: ENGAGE FEEDBACK SUPPORT TEAM

With the goals established and fully supported by the executive sponsor, the next stage is the Stakeholder Feedback Interview or gathering data on observed behaviors through participant interviews. The section that follows details the various steps in that process.

Stage Three. Process Step a. Set process overview and protocol:

Review the sub-steps of the Stakeholder Feedback Interview.
Prepare the Stakeholder Feedback Interview Protocol.

The feedback interview protocol consists of two parts. The first part follows a force field format, in which the interviewer seeks behaviors that both drive and restrain achieving the goal. Kurt Lewin advanced the seminal work in this area,[3] and training in Systems Centered Therapy[4] breathed life into my use of this tool. While focusing on the driving forces is important, often it is easier to cause change by focusing on the restraining forces—on what is getting in the way. The second part of the interview is derived from the powerful applied research of Jon Zenger and Joe Folkman.[5] They found that having more profound strengths and fewer career derailers separated those leaders who got promotions from those who didn't.

Although the Stakeholder Feedback Interview was described during the initial selection interview, a review of the process is helpful to orient the executive and guide this next phase of coaching. Each of the sub-steps are reviewed, with particular attention on the actions required by the executive. The interview protocol is the script that the coach uses to ensure consistent and comprehensive interviews. (The Stakeholder Feedback Interview Protocol is available in Appendix B.)

STAGE THREE: ENGAGE FEEDBACK SUPPORT TEAM	
PROCESS STEP	**DESCRIPTION**
a. Set process overview and protocol.	Review the sub-steps of the Stakeholder Feedback Interview. Prepare the Stakeholder Feedback Interview Protocol.
b. Identify feedback providers.	Carefully identify six to eight participants who have relevant knowledge of the executive's behavior and whose feedback the executive trusts.
c. Interview feedback providers.	Conduct a thirty-minute phone interview with each of the feedback providers to gather anchored feedback.
d. Analyze interview data.	Synthesize the individual reports, looking for themes and patterns.
e. Review written reports.	Review both the synthesized report and the detailed interview reports with the executive.
f. Engage in reflection and absorption.	Provide time for the executive to read the reports in detail and absorb the information.
g. Thank and engage participants.	Thank those who participated and set the stage for their continued engagement.

Stage Three. Process Step b. Identify feedback providers:

Carefully identify six to eight participants who have relevant knowledge of the executive's behavior and whose feedback the executive trusts.

The coach gathers feedback data through one-on-one interviews. The executive and coach identify six to eight people who will be invited to participate in the feedback interviews. Each interview takes thirty minutes to conduct and an additional thirty minutes for the coach to write up, so the desire to have more feedback should be balanced with the amount of coaching time available. The stories and insights garnered from these interviews are so cogent that carefully selecting key participants is more important than having a large number of participants. Of course, the term *360 degrees* comes from soliciting feedback from people on all sides of the recipient—direct reports, peers, and bosses—so representatives of all of those categories are ordinarily included.

There are three criteria for inclusion into the participant feedback pool:

- The executive is confident that the participant has her best interest at heart
- The participant has firsthand, contemporary knowledge of the executive's behaviors
- The participant is willing to share insights relative to the specific goals, whether favorable or otherwise

Reaching the objective of receiving actionable feedback depends on the executive trusting that the feedback participants have good intentions. This may eliminate some people who are in a politically sensitive situation within the organization or with the executive because of a recent incident.

Additionally, participants need to have firsthand knowledge of the executive's behavior, in order to provide valuable input.

Contemporary knowledge is preferred—the more recent, the better. In cases where the client has had a turn in careers, where she was perceived as being great in one role and then as being at risk of career derailment in the next role, there can be value in gaining insights by including feedback participants from both positions. It will help the coach determine whether the issue is with the executive's skills or the change in circumstances.

The third criteria, willingness to share, taps into the executive's knowledge of which people think independently and which will share their views candidly. As one executive put it, "No one on this list will blow sunshine at you." That approach to constructing the interviewee list is much preferred to including a good friend who will not offer any restraining forces—who only blows sunshine. The Stakeholder Feedback Interview process does not assume all direct reports are included or that all inputs are equally weighted.

The executive shares her involvement in a coaching process with the selected participants and obtains their agreement to schedule an interview with the coach. Participation is presented as a voluntary activity, not a positional power-driven obligation. This process helps executives regain or practice the spirit of asking for support and assistance from others. And it works because the executive only includes those who have her best interests at heart. In return, those whom the executive invites into this process are asked to do so by offering candid insights that they are willing to own. The value of the stories and insights these participants offer is paramount to the process. When we ask for targeted feedback, we make ourselves vulnerable; when we offer candid feedback, we make ourselves vulnerable. This process honors that for the true gift it is.

Stage Three. Process Step c.
Interview feedback providers:

Conduct a thirty-minute phone interview with each of the feedback providers to gather anchored feedback.

In introducing the interview plan to the feedback participants, the coach fosters safety, an environment that supports caring authentic disclosure, in several ways.

Boundaries are set on all facets of the conversation and include the following elements that build safety:

- *Empowerment.* Inviting the participants to share candid information demonstrates that their perspectives are valued.
- *Time boundaries.* Thirty-minute conversations honor the participant's time constraints and keep the dialogue concise.
- *Topic focus.* Participants are asked to give feedback pertinent to the executive's indentified goals and are redirected to those goals should they drift into other topics.
- *Specificity.* The interviewer is looking for descriptions of specific relevant behaviors rather than judgments or general impressions.
- *Examples.* Participants are encouraged to provide specific stories that illustrate their perspective and anchor the feedback for the executive.

- *Systems perspective.* Behaviors are categorized in relation to the goal as either driving forces or restraining forces, so that the effect on the system is considered.

At the end of each interview, the coach adds a safety net by re-testing the participant's consent for the coach to share his interview notes with the executive. If the interviewee used a particularly harsh word or attribution, the coach may revisit that and ask if the interviewee would like to rephrase the comment. Chapter 6 details interviewing techniques and strategies to guide interviewees away from judgments and toward observable behaviors, to manage the time, and to elicit further elaboration of observations.

The coach conducts the interview by phone, as this enables the coach to take detailed notes without worrying about the socially appropriate amount of eye contact. The coach relies exclusively on the notes, most often taken on a laptop throughout the interview.

The coach edits the phone interview notes immediately after the interview to ensure freshness of memory. Ensuring that the reports make sense and read well, including correcting the grammar, typically takes another thirty minutes, making it logistically easy to schedule the interviews on the hour.

The Stakeholder Feedback Interview Protocol begins with the coach's explanation of the interview process and includes the following core questions:

- *Driving and Restraining Forces.* For each goal statement, what are the (a) driving forces, behaviors that help the executive achieve the goal, and (b) restraining forces, behaviors that hinder the executive from achieving the goal?

- *Impact of Behavior.* What was the impact of that behavior on you? (When appropriate, this is asked as a follow up question on the driving or restraining forces.)
- *Profound Strengths.* What are the things the executive does that might be considered a profound strength, something in the top tenth percentile?
- *Career Derailers.* What are the things the executive does that might develop into career derailers or things that might prevent the executive from being successful in the current role?
- *What Else.* What else would be helpful for the executive to hear?

(The Stakeholder Feedback Interview Protocol is available as Appendix B.)

Gathering feedback that is anchored in behaviors and relevant to the goals is a primary objective of the interviewing activity. At times, this requires a disciplined approach to push past judgments and conclusions of the interview subjects and get to the underlying examples that will be meaningful for the executive. When the coach does not maintain that discipline, the feedback process is compromised.

The feedback generated through this process is powerful and, if the disciplined process is not followed, can lead to regrettable and unintended consequences. The antidote is to follow the process of insisting on grounded feedback. When the coach's initial prompts for grounded feedback go unheeded, there are still options. One is to reaffirm politely the need for grounded feedback. A higher level of intervention is to share that the inputs will be used for context, but that the coach will not be able to share that feedback with the client.

By this point, the coach may have used four levels of progressive insistence:

- Explaining the process at the beginning of the interview
- Asking for examples during the interview
- Reminding the person being interviewed of the power of having the feedback grounded
- Sharing the deficiencies of the use of non-grounded feedback

Stage Three. Process Step d. Analyze interview data:

Synthesize the individual reports, looking for themes and patterns.

The coach reviews the interview transcripts and looks for patterns and themes. Each transcript is seven to ten pages in length. The coach covers the broad themes and then supports those with comments from the interviews. The most telling anecdotes that support attributions lend powerful credibility and reduce deniability.

The coach prepares a Stakeholder Feedback Interview Summary Report. This report covers the themes for each goal, first providing the driving forces and then the restraining forces. Each theme is given a pithy title followed by the relevant quotes from those interviewed. While the themes carry greater weight, there are times that individual comments do not cluster into a theme but are worthy of inclusion in the summary. I list these under the heading "Important One-Off Comments."The sections "Profound Strengths" and "Potential Derailers" are so significant that rather than summarizing the comments, I typically include all of them. The coach also provides the executive with the typed notes from each interview. (The Stakeholder Feedback Interview Summary Report is available as Appendix C.)

Stage Three. Process Step e.
Review written reports:

Review both the synthesized report and the detailed interview reports with the executive.

The feedback summary report supplies insights on the future work of the coach and the executive. But first the executive has to be able to hear and absorb the feedback. The depth of the inputs from the support team and the care with which those insights were offered impress the executive and reduce defensiveness. One of the greatest impediments to the effectiveness of feedback is the readiness of the person receiving it to integrate and metabolize the new information into their existing schema or way of thinking. There are a number of things that go wrong. Everyone has observed those who are clever at finding ways to discount or avoid undesired or unwanted feedback; it is like watching water roll off a well-waxed surface. Some of those strategies are explicit and well rehearsed, such as disqualifying the source, discounting the context, and turning a deaf ear. There are other strategies that might not be as conscious or deliberate, such as being overwhelmed by shame, daunted by the implications, or confused by not having a framework for contextualizing the information. Most of us have experienced the rawness, and perhaps futility, of feedback given when we were not fully present or receptive.

A coach does not necessarily know how the executive is going to respond or which issues may cause defensive reactions.

Therefore, it is best to begin this process by sharing how much care and generosity the participants showed in responding. I have always been able to make this observation authentically; I am continually amazed by participants' thoughtful contributions. The executive's commitment to improve becomes apparent to the interviewees and elicits a positive response. Perceiving the participants' responses positively enables the executive to start the review with a sense of safety and befriending (elevated levels of oxytocin and endorphins) rather than a fight/flight or competitive reaction (pumping adrenaline and cortisol). Daniel Goleman, in his book *Emotional Intelligence*, coined the term *amygdala hijack* to describe the destructive cycle that can be triggered under stress.[6]

The coach can help clients manage the stress of receiving feedback and thus avoid this emotional hijacking. When something at the summary level does not fit well with the executive's self-perception, the coach can ground the comment with the specific statements and stories. At this point, the interview discipline of getting behaviorally anchored feedback yields high dividends; the coach has specific observations of behaviors that anchor the summary-level statements, rather than conclusions, attributions, or judgments. The feedback data, backed up with specific observations, makes a compelling case, one that is difficult to dismiss or deny.

In advance of our meeting, I include a cover letter with the report to the executive, offering suggestions for reading. Those include:

- Give yourself a quiet space and enough time to read this report without interruption.
- Read the thematic summary and individual interviews through once. Please do not speed-read or skim the good stuff!

- As you read the transcripts, pay attention to the positive driving-force statements people made, reading them at least once for every three times you read the restraining forces.
- As you read the restraining forces, remind yourself that this is exactly what you asked for.
- Read each item with an open mind. The participants offered the gift of sharing their perspective.
- Try to categorize the significant comments into four groups:
    - Yes: I can own that.
    - Maybe: I'll have to think about this feedback.
    - No: I do not own that.
    - So what? That is not important.
- Always consider that the feedback is offered with your best interests in mind.
- Finally, remember that these are the participants' impressions based on what they were paying attention to and are not necessarily who you are.

This juncture in the process is dependent on the deft coach's ability to prepare the executive to take in challenging feedback. Chapters 5 and 6 describe coaching skills that facilitate the acceptance of feedback.

The purpose of the feedback report is to shape the joint work of the coach and the executive, including building the Commit to Action Worksheet. It is highly recommended that the executive not share the feedback report with colleagues, as doing so could be viewed as a violation of the trust that was developed with the participants. The confidential nature of the feedback report was made known to the executive's sponsor/boss during the earlier goal alignment and support conversations.

Stage Three. Process Step f. Engage in reflection and absorption:

Provide time for the executive to read the reports in detail and absorb the information.

This process step was added to the model based on executives' comments on how helpful it was to spend time with the data, reading it, thinking about it, connecting it to their experiences. Executives are accustomed to moving through a lot of information fast. Discouraging that left-brained approach is likely to yield deeper insights. The richness of the stories and the personal level of sharing requires reflection. One of the benefits of the coaching engagement is supporting the executive in developing a reflective process. As one executive shared, "This is the only time I get to reflect." Part of the coaching experience is to model reflective thinking, contextualizing knowledge within a broader perspective. The executives who get the most out of the feedback share the common trait of making a personal commitment to understand the gift of feedback they have received.

Stage Three. Process Step g. Thank and engage participants:

Thank those who participated and set the stage
for their continued engagement.

Simple courtesy matters: we should thank those who help us. The most effective follow-up I have seen was an executive who set up short meetings with each participant and shared the value of one or two specific inputs. I recommend that the executive not share any partially formed action plans at this point but avert curiosity by saying she will be working on next steps with her coach. Ideally, these conversations will happen face-to-face in person, but if that's not possible, then face-to-face virtually or, as a last resort, by phone. Sending an email is not recommended because it feels too distant for the intimacy the participant shared and for building the support group the executive needs for sustained change.

The executive benefits by keeping some portion of the participants engaged as active feedback agents as the executive makes changes in her behaviors. These people know what she is working on and have already demonstrated a level of investment. The Seven-Stage Model builds on that; at the end of the coaching engagement, the executive goes back to these people and asks for feedback on her progress.

STAGE FOUR: COMMIT TO ACTION

STAGE FOUR: COMMIT TO ACTION	
PROCESS STEP	**DESCRIPTION**
a. Prioritize efforts.	Support the executive in deciding where to work. Guide the executive on clarifying criteria and linking back to the concurrent goals.
b. Draft key actions.	Identify key actions for each goal.
c. Select the action learning application.	Detail the action learning application where the executive will practice new behaviors.
d. Review the action plan for achievability.	Review the action plan, as a whole, to determine how much is achievable within the time of the coaching contract.
e. Formalize the committment.	Complete the Commit to Action Worksheet. Agree to use it to guide how coaching time is invested.

Once feedback has been analyzed and reviewed, the coaching engagement moves on to completing the Commit to Action Worksheet. This stage includes four critical components: (1) the key areas for behavioral development, the prioritization of efforts; (2) specific actions to take; (3) an action learning project; and (4) an action plan. At this stage, the one in which the executive makes commitments to changes in behavior, the potency of gathering behaviorally anchored feedback on the goals that are most important to the executive becomes apparent.

Stage Four. Process Step a. Prioritize efforts:

Support the executive in deciding where to work. Guide the executive on clarifying criteria and linking back to the concurrent goals.

The first process step at this stage is to guide the executive in identifying the key areas for behavioral development. These key areas are more apparent in some Stakeholder Feedback Interview Summary Reports than others. Coaching support is especially helpful with going from a massive amount of feedback data down to the few core areas—synthesized from the interview data—that offer the best pathway to goal achievement.

The report format used to guide this process starts with the restraining forces for a specific goal that were gleaned from the interviews. Most executives find that working on two or three specific behavioral changes for each goal meets the necessary test, the critical few things that have to be done if the executive hopes to achieve his goal. The sufficiency test, where executives look at what else would improve the likelihood of success, is more challenging, as most executives feel they are never doing enough and could always do more. Using criteria-based prioritization techniques ensures that the executive is clear on exactly why items are included or excluded. The coaching skills required for this facilitation are detailed in Chapter 6.

Stage Four. Process Step b. Draft key actions:

Identify key actions for each goal.

With a clear sense of the behaviors that constitute the most significant restraining forces, the executive and coach begin to develop a behavioral change program. Uncovering what the executive is willing to commit to doing to change behaviors is integral to developing the plan. Each specific restraining behavior is paired with a specific antidote, the behavior to change. For example, the restraining force might be a tendency to interrupt others with the resulting loss of their ideas and a residual feeling of disrespect, or a tendency to get bored and start scanning emails during a conversation. For each of these, the specific antidote behaviors that are acceptable to the executive are identified. The more specific the behaviors identified in the interview process are, the more specific the behaviors targeted as antidotes can be.

I find it important to challenge the executive's reflective thinking in the action planning segment by asking several core questions:

- What is the impact of your current behavior?
- Why would you be tempted not to change or value continuing as is?
- How will you catch yourself when repeating the old pattern?
- What will you do differently?

These questions are designed to encourage reflection. For example, is the impact of the behavior related to brand, reputation, morale, efficiency, or risk mitigation? When asking about the temptation to not change, the soft hypothesis is that the undesired behaviors may have been developed for good reasons. Maybe those reasons are no longer present. A template of the probes under each of these questions is included in Appendix A in the Commit to Action section.

There are more complex issues, where determining the most efficacious behavioral changes requires a comprehensive knowledge of leadership topics. This is why executive-level coaching requires a deep toolkit and knowledge base. With one executive, the restraining force that emerged was the feedback participants' frustration with the executive taking sides and showing favoritism. Since multiple people said the same thing, it was a pattern. My working hypothesis was that there was a group dynamic and that this was a system-level issue. The coaching work was based on knowledge from those two disciplines (group dynamics and systems thinking) to more deeply understand the issues and to devise the best behavioral change intervention. The International Coaching Federation[7] and other coaching affinity groups cover broad competency skills required of coaches. Research on the competencies coaches must possess to be effective in their role is ongoing, reflecting the evolving sophistication of coaching.[8] Chapter 5 covers broad skill areas that I find especially useful.

An integral component of the Seven-Stage Roadmap is a clear methodology for measuring success. The goals were structured to include a desired business or organizational outcome, such as increasing the effectiveness of the executive team by pushing decisions to the lowest appropriate level. This goal provides a specific behavioral action to be measured: Has the executive pushed decision making to the lowest appropriate level? The Seven-Stage Roadmap includes metrics that match the scope of the goal. Frequently, the best approach to gaining insight on the effectiveness of the changes is also the most straightforward: ask if the change has been made. The key value of this portion of the Seven-Stage Roadmap is building the expectation that progress will be measured and that there is a way to build accountability into the coaching design. (The Seven-Stage Roadmap worksheets are available in Appendix A.)

Stage Four. Process Step c.
Select the action learning application:

Detail the action learning application where the executive will practice new behaviors.

An action learning application provides a specific contained environment where the executive can practice the new behaviors. This makes the change process more accountable and improves the odds of success and the likelihood of seeing results from the coaching. The accountability increases with disciplined boundaries placed on the situation and surrounding circumstances in which the new behavior will be practiced. For example, at Monday morning staff meetings, the executive will be doing three things differently: (1) starting with an agenda, (2) making sure everyone participates, and (3) summarizing actions to be taken. When the executive takes the additional step of sharing these three behaviors with trusted colleagues who will be at the meeting, there is fast and accurate feedback available on how well he did. This step builds one of the powerful system-level benefits of the Seven-Stage Model by enhancing the usable feedback in the system.

Stage Four. Process Step d.
Review the action plan for achievability:

Review the action plan, as a whole, to determine how much is achievable within the time of the coaching contract.

The manageability of the overall Commit to Action Worksheet is tantamount to success. Executives have a wonderful capacity for trying to get everything done at once. Personal behavioral change takes the same dedicated level of attention and commitment as a doctor-monitored program of losing 10% to 15% of your body weight. The coach provides the balancing feedback loop by testing the realism of the Commit to Action Worksheet when viewed as a whole. Rarely are the components equally weighted.

Stage Four. Process Step e.
Formalize the commitment:

Complete the Commit to Action Worksheet.
Agree to use it to guide how coaching time is invested.

The Commit to Action Worksheet provides both the coach and the executive with a roadmap of where they are going. Seeing the whole map provides comfort that the coaching process will get the executive along the path to where he needs to be by the end of the coaching engagement. This is strategic. The coach is asking the executive to trust him that this process will work, that at the end of the day the outcomes will be achieved. To extract the full measure of the executive's motivation, he must believe in the likelihood of achieving the targeted outcomes. A written plan has the powerful benefit of keeping efforts on target while authorizing the coach to hold the executive accountable for the use of time and the prioritization of effort. For example, at the end of each month, the coach can check in with a snapshot look at how the executive is advancing against the overall plan and thus avoid any tendency to drift into the weeds.

The hard work of coaching takes place between the fourth stage and the fifth stage, between committing to actions and measuring success. The client has a clear set of goals, feedback on how their behaviors are helping and hurting in attaining those goals, and specific actionable plans on how to change. The success of a coaching engagement is deeply dependent on the diligence of the client, with support from the coach, on following through on those action plans. The action plan is a living document, one that is adapted and changed in an iterative fashion as the client and coach ascertain what is working and what is not working. New actions are added and old ones refined. Small successes are gleaned so they can be expanded on.

Just past the midpoint in the contract, the coach requests a three-way meeting with the client and the manager. The outcome objectives are to affirm the goals, to identify progress on those goals, to make midcourse adjustments if necessary, and to create an opportunity to keep the sponsor involved and engaged. These meetings often add a level of energy to the coaching engagement, reaffirming the importance of the goals to all parties.

STAGE FIVE: MEASURE SUCCESS

STAGE FIVE: MEASURE SUCCESS	
PROCESS STEP	**DESCRIPTION**
a. Decide when to measure.	Gather results approximately one month prior to the end of the coaching contract.
b. Determine what to measure.	Measure each goal, whether the executive thinks they made substantive progress or not.
c. Teach how to measure.	Transfer the knowledge of how to gather valid, usable feedback from the coach to the executive.
d. Report on progress.	Prepare the feedback on progress as a report that enables pre and post comparisons to the original feedback inputs.

The Seven-Stage Roadmap includes a worksheet on measuring success. The process of measuring the results occurs in the last month of the coaching engagement and provides three benefits. First, the executive gets the training necessary to replicate the feedback-gathering process. Second, the results are folded into the leading-edge issues for continued attention by the executive. Third, the accountability aspect of the process is reinforced. The outcomes of this measurement process should be available for review as part of the closure activities at the end of the coaching engagement. The executive is able to draw from this data in the final meeting with the coach, the executive, and the executive's sponsor. The coach is able to use this data should the organization request a final written report.

Stage Five. Process Step a. Decide when to measure:

Gather results approximately one month prior to the end of the coaching contract.

About one month before the end of the contract, the executive gathers updated feedback by repeating the participant interviews, using the same protocol that was used for the first interviews. This provides enough time for the executive to learn the process and for the coach and executive to review the results and refine the Commit to Action Worksheet as needed.

Stage Five. Process Step b. Determine what to measure:

Measure each goal, whether the executive thinks they made substantive progress or not.

The measurements are driven by the goals. The original interview process is repeated; the behaviors that support goal achievement (driving forces) are identified, as are the behaviors that deter or undermine goal achievement (restraining forces.) The measurement is a comparison of those driving and restraining behaviors recorded for each goal at the beginning of the coaching process to those recorded near the end of the coaching process.

Stage Five. Process Step c. Teach how to measure:

Transfer the knowledge of how to gather valid, usable feedback from the coach to the executive.

To bring closure to our coaching engagement, I ask the client to conduct a Mini–Stakeholder Interview in the last month of the engagement. The coach and client use the results to compare to the initial Stakeholder Interviews. A template of the Mini–Stakeholder Interview is included in Appendix E.

The underlying structure of the measurement process for the Mini–Stakeholder Interview is the same as that used in the Stakeholder Interviews at the beginning of the engagement, with several important changes. First, for parsimony on the expenses, the interviews cover half the number originally interviewed. Selecting this reduced pool has proven to be well received and fairly straightforward, since the supportive feedback relationships tend to deepen unevenly. The client knows who will tell them what they are looking for. Second, the client will be conducting the interviews. The process of allowing the executive to conduct the interviews continues to build openness and trust in the relationships between the executive and the feedback participants. These are the same participants who gave the original feedback, have been giving feedback on various action learning projects, and have been active participants on the executive's team to support making the targeted changes.

I work with the client to build an interview protocol. This approach builds on Stephen Finn's Therapeutic Assessment model,[9] in which he found that involving the clients in articulating the questions they wanted answered had positive outcomes on the engagement, relationship, self-esteem, and hopefulness variables. That joint exploration and self-empowerment is also at the core of Edgar Schein and Peter Schein's book, *Humble Inquiry*.[10] These conversations build engagement among the support team that can later be used to ensure that any backsliding behaviors are quickly brought to the attention of the executive. This is discussed further in the Sustain Progress section below.

Stage Five. Process Step d.
Report on progress:

Prepare the feedback on progress as a report that enables pre and post comparisons to the original feedback inputs.

The executive will have detailed notes from these interviews, and the coach will help the executive synthesize those into themes for comparison to the original interview results. These comparisons, anchored in behaviors, allow all parties to acknowledge the impact of the changes in behavior. These comparisons also allow the coach and the executive to target areas for additional effort.

STAGE SIX: SUSTAIN PROGRESS

STAGE SIX: SUSTAIN PROGRESS	
PROCESS STEP	**DESCRIPTION**
a. Recognize gains and opportunities.	Acknowledge progress and test for sufficiency.
b. Assess the risk of backsliding.	Discuss the assimilation level of the new behaviors and the context that may trigger old behaviors.
c. Identify additional actions.	Amend the Seven-Stage Roadmap as appropriate.
d. Engage with the executive sponsor.	Review progress with the executive sponsor: acknowledge gains, identify areas for continued focus, and secure ongoing support.

Most models of change include some variation of internalizing the change to ensure that gains last.[11] It's like learning to drive a car: experienced drivers know that reusing skills helps us apply them without a lot of conscious decisions. The second concept that cements the gains is institutionalizing. Experienced leaders know that building the culture that supports and reinforces the desired behaviors creates an environment that makes it easy to do the right things consistently.[12]

Stage Six. Process Step a. Recognize gains and opportunities:

Acknowledge progress and test for sufficiency.

The use of a pre and post comparison provides objective inputs on progress. This enables the executive to move beyond what he thinks to what others observe. There is an expected lag time between when someone begins making a change and when others notice a behavioral shift. The coach may caution the executive not to overreact when at first constituents don't notice progress. Consistency of action is paramount. On the other side—the risk of under-reacting—the coach can test if the Seven-Stage Roadmap activities were robust enough and whether the executive has achieved the level of improvement he had hoped for. In the former, the call to action is consistency of behaviors; in the latter, the call to action is adding activities to achieve greater impact.

Stage Six. Process Step b.
Assess the risk of backsliding:

Discuss the assimilation level of the new behaviors and the context that may trigger old behaviors.

From a systems perspective, one of the easiest errors is to assume that change is permanent. This coaching model starts from a healthy awareness of impermanence, a central concept of Buddhism. In a candid conversation, the coach and executive anticipate where the executive will experience a pull back to old behaviors. They identify the triggering events and have strategies in place to handle choices down the road. One of the recommended strategies is to make it easy for members of the team that have been providing the executive behavioral feedback to continue to do so, especially when they observe backsliding behaviors.

Stage Six. Process Step c.
Take additional actions:

Amend the Seven-Stage Roadmap as appropriate.

The Seven-Stage Roadmap, updated for changes (both for progress achieved and for new areas of focus) can serve as an easy reminder for the executive on the continued work—that the work was not a simple coaching engagement of some limited number of months, but rather a long-term commitment to increase leadership effectiveness. The goals include achieving business results, addressing leadership challenges, and developing a professional career. Those issues are ongoing, as is the Seven-Stage Roadmap.

Stage Six. Process Step d.
Engage with the executive sponsor:

Review progress with the executive sponsor: acknowledge gains, identify areas for continued focus, and secure ongoing support.

The executive sponsor has provided support and alignment throughout the coaching engagement. His involvement at this stage ensures continuity of that effort and ongoing support. There is also a pragmatic element. The sponsor can have a significant influence on the executive's career.

STAGE SEVEN: PROVIDE FEEDBACK TO COACH

STAGE SEVEN: PROVIDE FEEDBACK TO COACH	
PROCESS STEP	**DESCRIPTION**
a. Conduct an evidence-based coaching evaluation.	Create the space and process for the client to provide feedback.
b. Have conversations.	Engage the executive in the art of providing feedback.
c. Reflect and take action.	Metabolize the feedback into the coaching model.

Using feedback for development is at the heart of the Seven-Stage Model, and that principle applies equally to the executive and the coach. We begin this feedback loop with the Midpoint Coaching Evaluation. At approximately the midway point in the engagement, the coach sends the executive a questionnaire. I have found that relatively few clients complete the entire form. Rather, they will identify one or two things they want to talk about, which is perfect. This is a great way to empower the client and ensure that any expectation differences get resolved.

Prior to the last meeting in the coaching engagement, the coach sends the executive the End-of-Engagement Coaching Evaluation to solicit the same type of feedback he has been espousing. The evaluation covers the things the coach is expected to do well, the outcomes the executive experienced, and a section on surprises and particularly noteworthy insights.

Stage Seven. Process Step a.
Conduct an evidence-based coaching evaluation:

Identify the most important information.

Coaches benefit from articulation of the standards to which they hold themselves accountable and the outcomes they expect from a coaching engagement. Gathering information on these standards and outcomes provides the foundation for the evaluation of the coach. (The Evidence-Based Coaching Evaluation is available as Appendix D.)

Stage Seven. Process Step b.
Have conversations:

Engage the executive in the art of providing feedback.

The executive has been receiving feedback throughout the engagement, experiencing the recipient side, and now has the opportunity to practice giving feedback. This also provides an opportunity for the coach to model receiving effective feedback. The coach holds himself in a learning posture, seeking understanding of the links between behaviors and outcomes.

Most executives are willing to have this thirty-minute discussion in person during the time they have scheduled for coaching. In dialogue, the executive and the coach review the feedback instrument.

Stage Seven. Process Step c.
Reflect and take action:

Metabolize the feedback into the coaching model.

The Seven-Stage Model is, in large part, the product of the feedback from clients over the past two decades. Its various phases have been shaped by executive feedback on what worked and what did not work. For example, the feedback form was adapted to capture those "ah-ha moments." Clients shared how certain things were catalysts, giving them a new way of approaching things or new insights. They wanted me to capture these because they meant so much to them. And I wanted to capture those moments as part of my continuing quest to more deeply understand what executive coaches do that really matters.

Chapter Five

Coaching Skills for Building Relationships

The Seven-Stage Model is relationship-based both because it enriches executives' relationships within their organizations and because the transformative potential of the model is enlivened by the quality of the coach-executive relationship. This chapter highlights the relationship components that enable the executive to trust that the coach has created a safe place to do the work, an environment that facilitates change. Chapter 6 explores the process enablers that build the coach's competence with using the model.

There is a substantive and growing body of research that recognizes the quality of the coach-executive relationship as one of the factors that most reliably predicts the success of a coaching engagement.[1] This research is supported by my personal experiences and by the formal feedback gained from my clients. The desired relationship is much more than feeling good and getting along well. Rather, the relationship creates the containment space that provides sufficient safety and trust for the executive to engage in the process of coaching with the curiosity to grow and expand his leadership capabilities.

Whether the executive enters into the coaching engagement for developmental or reparative reasons, he will have some level of anxiety from fear of exposure, and this can be expressed as vigilance, defensiveness, or protectiveness as to the potential personal risks. Most common is the feeling of vulnerability when asked to share work-related performance information that might expose weaknesses. Without confidence in the credibility and competence of the coach, the executive will not have the level of trust necessary to feel sufficiently safe to share the information that is vital for the coach to know. As explicated in The Hierarchy of Sustained Change (see Figure 1 on page 12), the executive will not be able to turn off the normal defenses he maintains without a sense of safety and thus will not be able to fully access and engage the curiosity it takes to change and grow. The trust research suggests that this reality is scalable from close personal relationships to societal relationships to international relations.[2]

Most of us have had experiences in which we found ourselves guarded or defensive. When I get defensive, three things happen: (1) I lose about 30 IQ points; (2) my problem-solving creativity disappears; and (3) I become self-centric, turning my energy to protecting myself. My experience with the executives I coach has revealed something similar: when their energy gets invested in a variety of defensive strategies, there is little creative energy left for exploring causality or options. We have all experienced the futility of arguing with someone who is just mad as hell (fight response), of trying work with someone who has avoidance down to a science (flight response), or of trying to engage with someone who looks like a deer in the headlights (immobilized). The likelihood of these unproductive outcomes places a special premium on the coach creating and managing safety in the environment and teaching the executive how to replicate such a setting in her work environment. By addressing the self-management needs of the coach, the Seven-Stage Model changes the probability tables, shifting the odds toward the favorable outcomes that derive from the coach and the executive having full access to their resources by being open, curious, and willing to accept appropriate levels of vulnerability and risk taking.

The key coaching self-management skills that create and maintain the containment space for relationship are (1) the ability to connect with another person through empathetic attunement, experience, and subgrouping; (2) the mindfulness and self-awareness required to avoid judgments, attributions, and inferences; (3) the self-compassion to know how to accept our humanity without lowering the bar on outcomes; (4) the authenticity and congruency to say what needs to be heard while staying in relationship; and (5) the perspective of multiple roles to keep vigilantly focused on the executive's goals.

KEY COACHING SELF-MANAGEMENT SKILLS	
SKILLS	**DESCRIPTION**
1. Attuned Empathy	See the world through the executive's experiences.
2. Self-Awareness	Avoid judgments, attributions, and inferences.
3. Self-Compassion	Accept our humanity without lowering the bar on outcomes.
4. Authenticity	Say what needs to be heard while staying in relationship.
5. Multiple Roles	Keep a vigilant focus on collaborating on the executive's goals from a partner-observer-researcher stance.

SKILL ONE: ATTUNED EMPATHY

See the world through the executive's experiences.

Years ago, when I trained to facilitate executive-level group meetings as part of the Executive Committee (which is now Vistage, Inc.), their emphasis was on being eyeball-to-eyeball and shoulder-to-shoulder with the executives, so they sought out former executives to lead their groups. The Executive Committee believed that the executive group facilitators needed a skill set that inspired an executive to say, "This is someone I can work with, someone who understands my world." While that facilitation model does not require the complexity of a coaching model, their conclusion was valid then and is valid now;

executives are comfortable working with someone who understands their world. Experientially based empathy enables the coach to identify with and understand the executive's feelings or difficulties because of a kindred set of experiences that informs the empathy.

Attuned empathy is at the heart of building connected relationships.[3] When a coach is interviewing a potential client, that executive is constantly scanning for suitability of fit and chemistry, in order to determine whether he wants to work with this particular coach. As I listen to the reasons the executive wants to engage a coach, I look for opportunities to build what Yvonne Agazarian, in *Systems-Centered Therapy for Groups*, refers to as a "subgroup," a connection through joining the executive on his issue and then building on it through the coach's experience.[4] Providing an empathetic response enables the executive to see the similarities with another person and increases a sense of attunement. We empathetically engage others regularly when we signal attunement through common nonverbal (e.g., head nodding) and subverbal (e.g., uh-huh) behaviors.

The coach further demonstrates attunement by tracking the client's experience. This requires the coach to enter the client's world without preconceived ideas and is validated when the client acknowledges that the coach sees his world. During the initial interview, one prospective client was describing the challenges he was facing with another executive. The story made such sense to me that I got ahead of the executive and asked what happened in an area he had not yet talked about. He stopped, looked at me, and asked how I knew that had happened. I was so experientially attuned to his story that I was anticipating—in this case correctly. While it is never a good idea to finish sentences or leap ahead of your client, this executive later shared that my resonance with and understanding of his situation was the reason he selected me as his coach. Stated differently, my empathetic attunement was sufficiently high for him to feel understood; it was a central part of what he needed to take the risk to disclose potentially embarrassing information.

The early work in building a relationship between the coach and the executive provides a foundation for the entire coaching engagement. When the coach demonstrates consistency in being aware of and sensitive to the challenges facing the executive, the pool of trust deepens, which in turn leads to a greater willingness on the executive's part to discuss the real issues and address the challenges he faces with curiosity.

SKILL TWO: SELF-AWARENESS

Avoid judgments, attributions, and inferences.

The level of self-awareness required of coaches is substantial, as effectively serving the client is dependent on getting reality right—or, at least, you want to be in the vicinity. The coach is constantly making judgments on how to interpret information, when to ask for examples, when to push back, when to offer feedback, when to share insights, when to reframe the issue, etc. We human beings do some amazing mental gymnastics to make sense of our situations. We attribute motives, values, and beliefs to others. We quickly arrive at untested assumptions and inferences based on limited observations. Worse, when we cannot contain the thoughts or emotions that become stirred within us, we sometimes throw or project them out onto others. Basically, we are always striving to create a rational description of our world that fits with what we already "know." Coaches need self-awareness for the benefit of getting closer to an undistorted reality and to model behavior that encourages the executive to achieve further self-awareness.

Executives are moving fast and juggling a lot of demands on their time, and they are frequently asked to make decisions without certain knowledge, on limited information or observations. Time for reflection is one of the gifts of coaching, which is a nice way of saying executives do not have or take the time to reflect otherwise. The tendency of executives to jump on the first viable explanation, to move fast on scant information, and to push the edge with little time to reflect combines to make this group especially prone to unwarranted attributions and untested assumptions and inferences about their own behavior and the behavior of others. Coaches are not delivering their full value if they accept these attributions, assumptions, and inferences at face value. The coach's skill at keeping his own assumptions and inferences at bay affects his ability to get reality right just as much as his skill at recognizing the executive's assumptions and inferences.

My doctoral program gave me my first exposure to Chris Argyris, seminal thinker in the area of learning organizations and professor emeritus at Harvard Business School, and his Ladder of Inference.[5] Argyris presents a model, built like a simple stepladder, that describes how we sequence through a chain of inferences that appear perfectly reasonable to us but may not fit how another person sees things, much less how things actually are. We start by collecting data, then we select certain pieces of that data for attention, then we begin to make meaning of the data we attend to, and finally we draw conclusions. These conclusions help us modify or reaffirm our beliefs about how things work, which in turn support the actions we take. The reflexive loop in this model is a self-sealing argument: our beliefs about how things work influence the data we select, which often confirms those beliefs and prevent us from even seeing any disconfirming data.

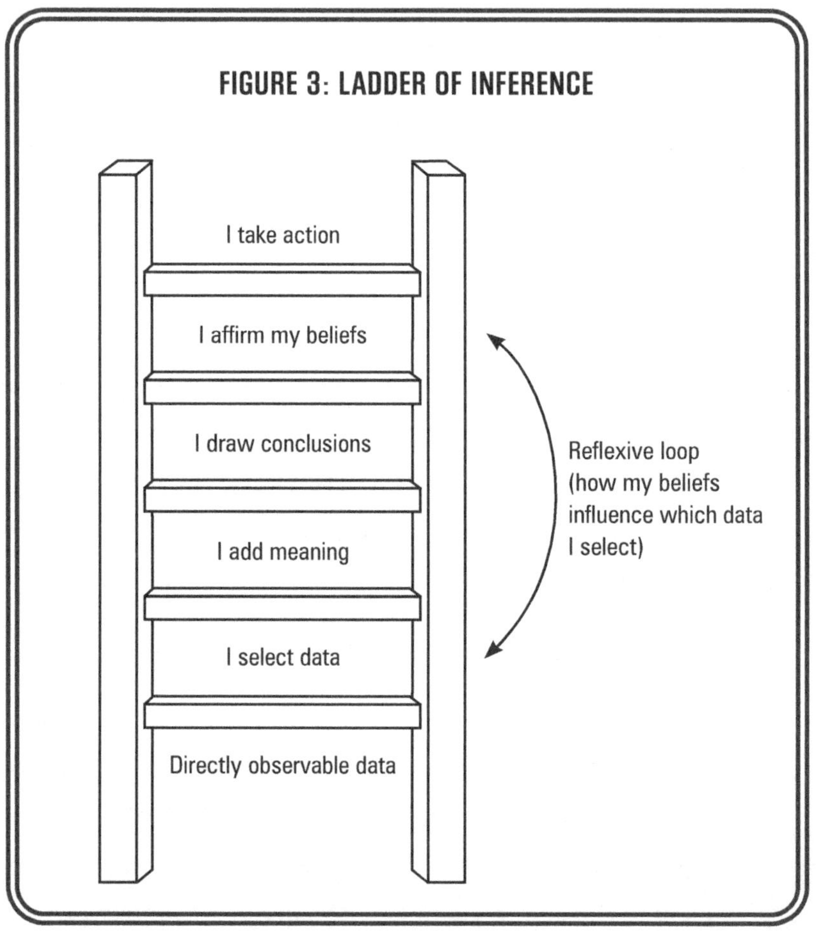

As I move up the ladder, developing my working hypotheses about what is going on, I hold those hypotheses softly, recognizing the risk of being too attached to them. An overconfidence bias about having reality right can prematurely block new and different information from being captured.[6] The reflexive loop aspect of the Ladder of Inference provides a great system-level view of how this works.[7] A strong belief can cause us to unconsciously filter the data we see such that the only data that hits our perception is that which supports our existing views, further solidifying that belief and making it even harder to be objective about new data.[8]

This tendency to see only what we are looking for is so pervasive that I adjusted how I teach topics on leadership to graduate students so that they can experience it firsthand. I now structure my case-study questions for the students by requiring them to reread the same case for each class, looking for data in support of the topics we are covering that week. The student reaction is consistently one of surprise. Although they have read the case a number of times, when they look for something specific as they read, they feel as if they had never seen that specific information before. This is confirmation that Argyris nailed it: we see what we are looking for. Staying open to new information is a discipline, one that serves coaches well in service to getting reality right or at least "in the vicinity of right."

An executive I coached struggled with how to work with fellow executives whom he perceived to have placed their personal career interests ahead of the best interests of the company. This tension spilled out as annoyance, which he channeled into tenacious challenges to the value of his colleagues' recommendations. As you can imagine, these challenges were not well received. After working with this client for a while, it became apparent that he carefully selected data that was aligned with his belief that his colleagues were self-serving and simply overlooked data that was disconfirming. While there were some self-serving behaviors influencing the organization, his emotional reaction to this one issue had distorted his perspective and impeded his effectiveness. When those he challenged became defensive, he perceived their reaction as further proof of his beliefs, leading to ever more ardent searching for confirming data. It is amazing to observe this phenomenon at close hand in others, and even more shocking to catch ourselves being blind to disconfirming data.

Experienced coaches recognize that the starting point the executive chooses may not be a presentation of the real issue. Clients need to affirm their safety and belief in the competency of the coach before they drop their shields and allow themselves to be authentic and vulnerable. When we feel unsafe, we tend to adopt defensive behaviors, which make us more likely to have negative attributions. When the coach holds fast to a view of what is going on, which can fall anywhere between a hard hypothesis and a pathological certainty, it does a disservice to the executive. The coach can get locked into a view that is not accurate and thus become less open to receiving information that would help formulate a more accurate hypothesis.

Another powerful tool for increasing self-awareness for the coach and the executive is reflection. As I was reviewing the impact of a coaching engagement with a client, she described how this was the only chance she had in years to thoroughly think through issues, to get a handle on where she was going, and make strategic choices about her professional development. This view on how precious it is to have a structured environment for deeper thinking and reflection has been echoed by many clients.

Fostering a habit of reflection gives coaches a more circumspect view of how their biases show up in coaching conversations. This increased awareness-through-reflection was reinforced by my work as a doctoral student, my training in group dynamics, my work with a personal master coach, and my training as a coaching supervisor. Each of these multiyear programs was based on reflective practices and required the discipline of taking time to reflect on the experiences to get the most from the learning opportunities they presented.[9] The discipline of self-awareness exhorts coaches to give themselves what they give their clients: the gift of perspective, the use of reflection to frame and reframe issues and understandings.

Another self-awareness facet that is essential to building the type of relationships that lead to success is ensuring my neutrality, getting my own stuff out of the way of the executive's story. At times, I would find my openness to an executive influenced by drama from another context, perhaps even from my own life, making me less than neutral and fully available. After attending a weeklong retreat led by Drs. Chris Germer and Bill Morgan in 2005, I began a mindful meditation practice to minimize my internal distractions and distortions.

Germer describes mindfulness as the moment-to-moment awareness that allows you to know what you are experiencing when you are experiencing it, without judgment.[10] My mindful meditation practice has helped me observe how my brain works, giving me the ability to stand outside myself and observe how I am thinking.[11] This amazing development has enhanced my ability to stay connected and attuned to my clients. This mindfulness meditation practice has been so helpful that I make a habit of arriving early for my appointments, perhaps sitting in the lobby, and taking five to ten minutes to reset my mind through a brief meditation.

In a book chapter on coaching self-management, Travis Kemp amplified this principle when he wrote, "As the coach's perceptual filters and processing biases are more mindfully managed within the coaching conversation, less data from the client's unique perspective and context is lost through the coach's filtering process and more richness from the client's own experience can be harnessed within the development."[12] This self-awareness through mindfulness supports other key coaching traits, including authenticity and congruency.

From almost the day I started coaching, I have been attending weekly sessions with my master coach to build my self-awareness. When I read an article that described the ideal master coach as someone who "is highly skilled in intrapersonal/interpersonal, psychological and developmental dynamics and is an experienced resource with extensive training in the helping professions,"[13] I wanted to shout, "That is who I have!" My commitment to the master-coach relationship tightly links to my goal of understanding how my personal issues and history influence my coaching. Coaches need a trusted external agent with whom they are willing to take the risk of being vulnerable in order to build self-awareness. The isomorphism is that by having a master coach we are practicing what we ask our clients to do in the coaching engagement.

The skill of self-awareness has significant influence on the other skills in this section. The five key disciplines detailed in this chapter build on each other. For example, I find that taking my authority as a leader, holding my space in a tough conversation, or articulating my values all take a level of moral courage that is grounded in self-awareness.

SKILL THREE: SELF-COMPASSION

Accept our humanity without lowering the bar on outcomes.

In the summer of 2011, I attended my third weeklong meditation retreat, this one led by Dr. Chris Germer, Dr. Bill Morgan, and Susan Morgan. Chris Germer had recently published *The Mindful Path to Self-Compassion*, in which he states, "The challenge is to turn toward our difficulties with non-judgmental awareness and compassion."[14]

This was my first introduction to including self-compassion into my mindfulness practice. While Chris is writing to the individual, I think this is perfect advice for the coach using techniques to improve self-awareness. The painful side effect of increased self-awareness is seeing our own foibles and shortcomings more vividly, but this side effect can be assuaged with self-compassion.

The more I am able to listen to my internal dialogue with non-judgmental awareness and compassion, the more I can externalize those qualities in my coaching conversations. The mindfulness and self-compassion aspects of meditation enhance the observing self and create internal space. There is a paradox in this process. In the Buddhist tradition, mindfulness and compassion are pathways to reduced suffering. However, most executives and coaches did not get to their current levels by setting the goal as reduced suffering, and, as I did, they may see it as a threat to maintaining their competitive edge. In fact, many executives believe they got to where they are by working hard (for most of them, very hard) and by driving themselves through the barriers. I appreciated one executive's philosophy of leadership that advocated, when given a fork in the road, to take the hard road. As with this executive, many of us are wired to enjoy the challenge. The paradox is that most of us do want to reduce suffering and yet believe a high inner drive for change is needed in order to achieve noble goals. In general, change theories propose that the chance for a change effort to be successful is related to the level of dissatisfaction or pain that exists as a reaction to the status quo. Some high achievers are afraid that compassion might turn into an overall mind-set of acceptance that results in passivity. I frame the challenge as being able to hold onto our inner drive for higher goals while being compassionate with our limitations and the discomfort those limitations induce.

Jim Fixx, the running guru, used to admonish serious runners about wearing headsets and listening to loud music as a means of distracting themselves from the inevitable pain of pushing to the next level.[15] He noted that world-class runners use their pain awareness to inform themselves of what is going on: they take alternative actions, sometimes adjusting their gait, sometimes driving through it, and sometimes just stopping. Similarly, in coaching, the goal is not to avoid pain and suffering or drive through it. The goal is to acknowledge it as feedback and to work with it in service to a higher-level goal.

Self-compassion enables one to fully embrace the personal discomfort of situations and then to make informed choices about how to behave instead of being unconsciously compelled by that discomfort. The pain that is not acknowledged does not disappear; rather it goes underground. Having self-compassion opens the door to greater insights so we can explore the ever-present barriers. The preliminary research supports that self-compassion actually frees one to take action by reducing the denial defense patterns and increasing awareness of the specific roadblocks to progress, and thus to reaching goals.[16] The coach uses compassion, along with the other tools, to expand the holding environment and thus increase the possibility for both the executive and the coach to tap their full resources for transformative solutions.

Publishing this book on transformational executive coaching is my testimony to this principle. My other two "books," one on mentoring and one on executive presence, reside on the top of my office filing cabinets as outlines, drafts, and piles of support articles. Until I acknowledged the specific restraining forces, the things that were causing me pain, I wasn't able to write a book. I was doomed to repeat the cycle until I owned my specific blocks. While in denial, I was not able to identify or directly address the issues and was certainly not in a position to devise creative alternatives and take the necessary constructive actions to achieve my goal.

With a deep belief in the need for self-compassion in service to uncovering the barriers to becoming our best selves, the coach brings this way of being present into the coaching relationship. As the executive takes small risks by bringing her real issues into the coaching conversation, the coach has the opportunity to reinforce this behavior by taking in the information without judgment and with an invitation for the executive to have some self-compassion.

As I listened to the story a client was sharing, it was clear she had good intentions and that the unintended consequences of her actions were significantly unfavorable. She had a desire to prevent a colleague in another department from making a serious mistake, but her choice of interventions proved to have incendiary consequences. As is often the case, everyone paid attention to the unintended impact rather than the good intentions. The perceived need to defend herself against this criticism was blocking access to recognition of her role in the situation. This denial of any wrongdoing presented an impermeable barrier to change. Until she could see the issue reframed and understand that her actions included both sincere caring and inappropriate boundary management, she was not able to hold enough self-compassion to drop the denial defense and move the coaching to the next phase.

SKILL FOUR: AUTHENTICITY

Say what needs to be heard while staying in relationship.

Authenticity is one of the underlying constructs of a leader with personal presence. In *Executive Presence*, Belle Halpern and Kathy Lubar define "leadership presence" as the ability to connect authentically with the thoughts and feelings of others in order to motivate and inspire them toward a desired outcome.[17] I modify this construct to read, "Coaching presence is the ability of the coach to connect authentically with the thoughts and feelings of the executive, in order to inspire and support them toward their desired outcome." Coaching is strongly aligned with Robert Greenleaf's vision of the leader as servant, as the coach works in service to the executive.[18]

Authenticity is about owning who you are and what you bring to the table. Warren Bennis, in talking about leadership, says the point is to become yourself, to use yourself completely—all your skills, gifts, and energies—withholding nothing.[19] Effectiveness as a coach requires an internal conviction to bring ourselves to the conversation, to serve as a sounding board, as the neutral third party, and sometimes as the sanity check on reality. When we bring ourselves to the conversation, we make "I" statements, share our experience, and mirror back what we see and experience. This requires a full and unreserved commitment to service and the willingness to take the risk of being wrong or not fully appreciated in the moment. Coaching is not about being liked or morphing into whatever the coach thinks the client wants. It is about helping achieve the executive's goals, even when that means confronting the issues and holding her accountable to her commitments.

While completing a Stakeholder Feedback Interview, I gathered information from an executive's direct reports that I knew would be hard for him to accept. The feedback was harsh. It would have been easier for me to treat it as all third-party data without adding my own voice, reporting that, "This is what they said." But I had my own data. This executive could be a bear, with a challenging and in-your-face style. I captured his attention when I backed up the feedback data by sharing two specific examples from our interchanges where the same behaviors were present. He got it. This level of authenticity allowed him to ask me questions about exactly what he did that triggered those responses. Perfect! Authenticity created the opportunity for curiosity, reflection, and deeper understanding, which led to choices of alternative behaviors.

Being authentic has another side—being able to fully appreciate, validate, and honor our clients for who they are. There is so much delight in listening to clients' wonderful stories. While the stereotypical image of the executive is someone who lacks humility, my experience is quite different. Executives do many things well and a few things with true distinction. They often do not recognize or give themselves credit for those areas of special gifts. Being able to observe and honor their gifts introduces the joy of authentically celebrating successes.

Entering into coaching, like most consequential endeavors, is not for the faint of heart. We bring our unique selves to the table, which sometimes feels like the sacrificial altar. As Ralph Waldo Emerson in his 1841 essay "Self-Reliance" said, "There is a time in every man's education where he arrives at the conviction that envy is ignorance; that imitation is suicide; that he must take himself for better or for worse as his portion."[20]

Acting congruently is a by-product of being authentic. Being authentic is knowing ourselves and being ourselves as we engage with others, an absence of role playing or pandering to the expectations of others. Congruency refers to the alignment of thought, feelings, and actions. Russ Moxley expounds on congruence to include being transparent and matching inner reality with one's outward expression.[21] The key is to bring those thoughts, feelings, and interpretations into the coaching conversation while in relationship with the executive. Peter Block, in his highly acclaimed book, *Flawless Consulting*, said that authentic behavior with a client means you put into words what you are experiencing with the client as you work.[22] He believed this was the most powerful thing you could do to gain the leverage you are looking for and to build client commitment.

SKILL FIVE: MULTIPLE ROLES

Keep a vigilant focus on collaborating on the executive's goals from a partner-observer-researcher stance.

A coach effectively leverages the potential impact of the coaching engagement by adding the roles of observer and researcher. As an observer, the coach serves as the neutral outsider who can see the culture and actions, framing the issues to push the edges of awareness without getting pulled into that system. As a researcher, the coach contributes outside information and resources to increase understanding.[23]

Observer Role

Achieving results requires the coach to maintain a certain stance or distance that enables him to be an objective observer while still being deeply engaged. In social science research, this boundary-maintenance function is a crucial component of being a "participant-observer."[24] In coaching, I prefer to define this necessary balancing force as the "partner-observer" role. Too much partnership inappropriately shifts the coaching relationship to a friendship. While I deeply honor and enjoy my executive clients, they do not hire me because they need a friend. If the coach uncritically embraces the executive's perspective or story, the coach risks colluding with the executive in justifying existing attitudes and behaviors. Maintaining the partner-observer balance forms a creative tension in coaching. It is the depth and quality of the relationship (partner side) balanced by objectivity as the coach pushes for greater insights, challenges old perceptions, and insists on accountability (observer side) that enables sustained change.

Holding this partner-observer stance is challenging. The coach may become so empathetically attuned with the executive's worldview that his independent thinking is subjugated. This loss of boundaries around the coach's role causes the loss of the outsider's perspective and objectivity. Ironically, it is exactly this ability to enter from outside the system, without the organizational cultural filters, that enables the coach to see that world for what it is. The coach engages in a collaborative partnership while also maintaining a level of circumspection that allows for testing and challenging the way those within the system have framed issues.

I have been surprised by my accidental loss of neutrality. I was working with an executive who struggled with one small department where he felt the top two people were in over their heads. This department worked for him only indirectly, and due to internal politics, he felt he was not able to influence any personnel actions. His strategy of choice was to spend more and more time influencing the department's output. His actions made perfect sense to me, as in our conversations we were framing the issues in terms of protecting the interests of the company and compensating for a lack of competence. In a subsequent conversation, the CEO framed the issue differently; he thought the problem was my client's need for control. When I contemplated that my client may have an underlying issue with control, I had to question whether I had lost my neutral position and my objectivity by over-sympathizing with his frustration. This opened a productive conversation with my client and helped forge a stronger relationship.

Another aspect of the observer role is the coach's ability to see the foibles and idiosyncrasies of the organizational culture. Clients expect the coach to (1) observe the dynamics with an objective outside perspective, and (2) speak up authentically on those observations. The potency of the questions the coach asks derives from the lack of embedded assumptions about how things work. A neutral outsider does not take for granted the things an insider does. This objectivity enables the coach to work at a systems level, seeing the dynamics with greater objectivity. I had an interview for a coaching engagement that included a number of people but not the client, because the organization's top leaders felt the situation was messy and wanted to pre-assess the coaches invited to interview with the executive. As I listened with an observing stance, I was tracking the system, the interdependencies that the senior person was describing. About two-thirds of the way into the meeting, I offered to share what I was hearing. Because I was mapping the relationships, building patterns, and connecting the dots from outside their system, I was able to describe the situational dynamics in a way they had not considered. They decided to shift the coaching to a higher-level executive because of what appeared to them as new information.

Researcher Role

In addition to balancing the coach-executive partnership with an objective outsider's perspective, the coach adds value with a researcher's stance. In the researcher's role, the coach provides knowledge, insights, and resources. The coach brings rich context by accessing external information relevant to the situation, introducing creative approaches, and making new connections.

Books, articles, and job aids are all means of providing executives with additional information on a topic. Contemporary knowledge of issues and the commitment to ground comments in solid research builds credibility and thus efficacy. I sometimes provide a reprint of an article along with a summary of how I think it relates to our work. Working with one client led me to read a book on a narrow topic to help me better understand his behaviors and to ask better questions during our coaching sessions. For another client, I created a job aid that detailed the various decision-making strategies and how each of those entailed a trade-off between time invested and commitment to the decision. This job aid provided an easy format to discuss the pros and cons of each option.

Another coaching discipline that adds value is expanding the innovative and creative approaches applied to solving problems. Executives solve formidable challenges all day, and, like most busy people, they rely on tried-and-true methods. The coach has the opportunity to see the issues with fresh eyes and uncover innovative approaches. To avoid their own habitual solutions, coaches benefit from learning methods to increase their ability to think creatively.[25] The following five techniques spur my creative thinking while in the midst of coaching: (1) doodling, (2) divergent thinking, (3) jumping levels, (4) stakeholder analysis, and (5) soft hypothesis. While I've listed these as five separate techniques, in practice they feel like one unified process.

Doodling

When in conversation with executives I take notes that are more accurately "doodles" because, in addition to words, they include schematics, drawings, dots, connecting arrows, and so on. This process serves multiple purposes. It supports maintaining an observer stance by keeping me from becoming too engaged in the conversations, too caught up in the story. Second, it provides a loose record of the conversation to use later to review process, progress, and insights. Third, and maybe most important, it activates both the left and right side of my brain. Engaging both hemispheres of the brain provides access to different ways of processing information.

Divergent Thinking

With the right brain activated, divergent views emerge more easily. Simple questions (sometimes ones I ask myself) help uncover the views: "What else could be going on?" "How does that statement coexist with your last statement?" Playfully approaching conversations as puzzles or riddles to be solved keeps me open to the unexpected. I am actively looking for apparent contradictions, discrepancies, and redundancies—puzzle pieces that do not fit.[26] One executive I worked with shared that she had been critiqued as "not being sufficiently encouraging," but she had just told a story that included what I believed to be a set of encouraging behaviors. I expressed that apparent contradiction and my puzzlement over what I was missing. I wanted to know how we, in our partnership, would make sense of this difference. Putting the issue on the table opened a conversation on her values and provided insight into how she could improve the alignment between her values and behaviors.

Jumping Levels

The technique of jumping levels in the system reflects the coaching commitment to stay goal-focused, continually checking that the executive is working on the right goal, at the right level. The mind-set of the coach is to constantly scan and test whether there are other higher-level goals that are more engaging and impactful. The presenting issues might not be at the right goal level. For one executive, the presenting challenge was to improve his relationship with other executives. By being curious about and exploring if this was the right goal, why this was so important, and what he hoped to gain from having those relationships, our coaching conversations moved the goal to achieving success on a new corporate initiative. In a later coaching conversation, this goal morphed again. He came to believe that his higher-level goal was to own his personal authority and to be authentic in all relationships. This is quite different from a goal of changing one's style to fit that of the other person or to saying all that matters is getting the project done.

Stakeholder Analysis

The use of stakeholder analysis requires the coach to be curious about the perspective of the other affected parties. Creative geniuses and Nobel Prize–winning physicists Albert Einstein and Richard Feynman both used this technique in order to creatively gain elusive insights. This encourages the consideration of other possible interpretations of motives and intents. It is a reflective technique to recognize complexity and hold in check the tendency to take things personally.

Holding a Soft Hypothesis

The first four techniques lead to the final creativity-enhancing tool of holding a soft hypothesis. With a goal of getting reality right, the coach is constantly making and testing hypotheses about how to interpret what is going on. Sometimes simply asking clients for their insights or best guesses provides the needed perspective. At other times, the coach has a hypothesis that can be either directly voiced or used to guide the process of gathering additional information. Either way, the hypothesis should be held softly, as if it were a bird that is about to be set free. This stance honors the uncertainty and limited access to all relevant information, prevents a power struggle or defensiveness triggered by a coach presuming certainty, and reflects the coach's commitment to develop a shared interpretation, an attitude of exploring how the other person is right.[27]

Chapter Six

Coaching Skills for Sustained Change

The preceding chapter covered the transcendent coaching relationship skills that apply to all coaching activities. The effectiveness of the Seven-Stage Model requires practical skills specific to each stage, which are reviewed in this chapter. Because the ongoing and transformational benefits of enhancing the feedback environment distinguish the model, special emphasis is placed on the techniques and skills that facilitate that outcome.

PRIOR TO STAGE ONE

Preparing for the Selection Interview

Companies use two different approaches for assigning executive coaches. The approach usually preferred by multinational and Fortune

100 firms is a preapproved pool of qualified coaches that are vetted and coordinated either internally by the human resources or organizational development departments or externally through one of the large coaching firms with international reach, such as CoachSource, the Center for Creative Leadership, PDI Ninth House, Lee Hecht Harrison, or Right Management. As the firm's executives request or are nominated for coaching, the coordinating organization will select two or three potential coaches for the executive to interview. Most professionals in the field recognize the benefits of giving the executives a voice in choosing their coach. This gives them some "skin in the game" and, consequentially, a higher level of commitment and engagement.

The approach that suits many firms is using one coach or a small number of coaches to work with multiple members of the executive team. This approach provides the value of deep cultural awareness and gives the coach the ability to leverage organizational knowledge. When being considered as the coach that will work with multiple members of an organization, the coach should expect to be interviewed by a number of top executives, including the CEO.

There are skills in getting the contract, just as there are in a job interview, which of course is what this is. The prospective coach is interviewing for a contract to coach an executive for a relatively short period of time, six to twelve months.

Prior to an interview, I review what I know about the client in order to identify possible connections with my background. With one large organization, I was having a much higher interview conversion rate (percentage of executives selecting me as their coach to the number of selection interviews) than my peers. A colleague asked me what I was doing that might explain that difference. I described the process I used, and it quickly became obvious that others were not making the same investment. As with a job interview, the prospective coach sends a signal of commitment by demonstrating to the executive that she is willing to invest time in understanding the organization. I start by gathering publicly available background information on the executive's career, the key issues and challenges the business is facing, the management structure, and press coverage on the firm. I will talk with the coordinating contact to see what they can share about the type of coaching that might be desired, as well as precipitating events and known client issues. Coaching engagements are initiated for a variety of reasons—developmental, assimilative, corrective, or as part of a larger initiative. I then test this larger context against my background and experience. What do I have in common with this executive? What experiences do I have that may be relevant to this situation? I bring a readily accessible pool of information to the interview that I can use to build connections and thus leap-start the coaching.

Perhaps most importantly, I use the interview as an opportunity to model how I conduct myself as a coach. I ask for permission to discuss an issue that is important to the client. We explore how she is framing the issue, and I try to model the self-management skills identified in this chapter.

TRANSFORMATIONAL EXECUTIVE COACHING SEVEN-STAGE MODEL

STAGE	DESCRIPTION AND DELIVERABLE
1. Establish Relationship	Meet the executive, review the coaching process, and determine the mutual benefit of entering into a coaching contract. Clarify what it means to work in a safe, bounded, goal-directed relationship.
2. Frame Change Intent	Guide the executive in creating an explicit statement of three or four goals that have the full support of the executive's sponsor.
3. Engage Feedback Support Team	Conduct the Stakeholder Feedback Interviews. Review the goal-directed feedback report with the executive.
4. Commit to Action	Complete the Commit to Action Worksheet that includes (1) the key areas for behavioral development, (2) specific actions to create change, (3) an action learning project, and (4) an action plan.
5. Measure Success	At approximately five months into a six-month coaching engagement, the executive asks the same feedback support team to reevaluate the driving and restraining forces to his goals.
6. Sustain Progress	Meet with the executive and the executive's sponsor to provide a high-level overview of progress and to build ongoing support from the sponsor.
7. Provide Feedback to Coach	The executive evaluates the coach against goals that were important to the coach.

STAGE ONE: ESTABLISH RELATIONSHIP

The Selection Interview

The coach should expect to propose an agenda for the selection interview. As described in Chapter 4, I break the meeting into three segments. The first two segments are straightforward information sharing by each party, with a good dose of building rapport and establishing professional credibility and as much subgrouping as is possible. The coach uses this portion of the conversation to gain clarity on the relevant business issues and the leadership challenges faced by the prospective client. In order to gain a perspective on how the executive sees the coaching engagement, the coach asks the executive what he wants to achieve and what led to requesting a coach at this particular time.

The third segment can take radically different paths, depending on whether the potential engagement is developmental or corrective. In a developmental engagement, the executive is generally positive and upbeat about the opportunity and excited about beginning. In the corrective or issue-specific engagement, the executive is generally more restrained and may be hesitant to disclose genuine issues. He is starting with a low sense of safety and trust. These two situations will benefit from different coaching approaches and from coaching skills that can be demonstrated in the selection interview.

The Developmental Engagement: The High Trust and Safety Case

When the executive is in this positive energy space, the coach's goal is to provide a sense of what the coaching experience would be like. The coach begins by helping the executive move from business and leadership challenges to potential goals. The goal of this conversation is to demonstrate how the coach works and provide enough information about the coach and the model for the executive to make an informed choice about whether this is the coach to help him successfully identity and master the challenges he faces.

During a selection interview, as the executive and I completed the first two segments of the interview, sharing information and exploring business issues and leadership challenges, I asked how he rated himself on resolving some of those critical issues. He was adept at relating his sense of success across a multitude of business issues. I was curious about which ones were under control, with progress being made, and which ones were still stumping the organization. This curiosity translated into questions that nudged the executive into beginning the coaching process of making sense of why things got stalled in several areas. My work was to translate these issues into potential coaching goals. When he mentioned several times how dedicated selected members of his team were, I wondered about the specificity and asked if this sense of urgency was shared broadly across the organization. It most certainly was not! He gave a lengthy history of the problems in this area.

By following where he placed emphasis (the dedication of select members) and where he did not place emphasis, the white space (those not being included), I was able to articulate one of those questions that produce an "ah-ha moment." The executive formed a tentative goal of creating an environment with a shared sense of urgency. The technique of jumping to a systems level with a follow-up question to discover what is not included in a response is great for bringing deeper understanding to the surface. I was also scanning for linkages between business issues, leadership challenges, and career aspirations. When executives see these links, they claim ownership of the goal and thus unleash their motivation for the hard work of change.

During this conversation, the third segment of an hour-long conversation, we crafted three potential goals. I do not presume that the goals created in such a hasty manner will turn out to be the most salient goals. The drive for targeted action, especially when working with executives, has to be tempered with a level of circumspection. The coach cannot get caught up in a drive and optimism for positive outcomes, because at this juncture, not enough is known to allow the executive to jump definitively on the first set of goals that sound pretty good. That is okay because at this stage, the goal is just to give the executive enough information about the coach and the model to make an informed choice.

The Corrective Engagement: The Challenge of Low Trust and Safety

When the executive is in this negative energy space, the first task is to provide him with a sense of safety and trust. The coach's challenge is to recognize where the executive is and not push disclosure and risk taking until he signals a readiness to move forward. The good news is that the coach usually has enough information to know whether the engagement is developmental or corrective.

For one corrective engagement, the executive signaled discomfort by repeatedly asking questions about confidentiality. Until this issue was resolved satisfactorily in his mind, there was no further progress. If the coach misses the first cue, the executive will keep circling around until he gets it. In this case, sharing the examples of how I handled myself in other coaching cases where confidentiality mattered and was tested provided the comfort level the executive needed.

Another client signaled distress by asking to hold our conversations away from his office. The risk that his boss and colleagues would learn that he was receiving coaching caused him to take this atypical step. The regional operating group was not aware that someone at the corporate office had authorized the coaching. Our first conversations had to center on both confidentiality and logistics. His sense of safety increased as I shared the boundaries of confidentiality and the point at which I could no longer work with an individual. This touches on the coaching industry's code of ethics as well as personal integrity. For example, I will not continue to work with a client who has made a firm decision to leave the organization—the one that pays my bill. And yet talking about options and the pros/cons of leaving the organization can be a starting point of the coaching conversation and may enable the executive to move beyond the "grass is greener" lore and consider the hard work of changing behaviors.

There will be ample opportunity to address business issues, leadership challenges, and career aspirations during future conversations. If the coach does not create a foundation of safety and trust, he will not even get that opportunity.

STAGE TWO: FRAME CHANGE INTENT

With the contract approved, the first several coaching sessions frame the intention to change by honing in on the executive's critical goals. The following process skills enable the coach to expediently complete this work, which typically takes two or three sessions. The quality and relevance of the behavioral insights gained during the Stakeholder Feedback Interview process depend on the quality of the goals.

As with any project, setting high-quality goals is as much an art as a science, and there are many criteria for good goals. Within the context of the Seven-Stage Model, the criteria are to concurrently address the business issues facing the organization or division, the leadership challenges facing the executive, and the executive's career-development aspirations. This section on goal setting is for a developmental coaching engagement; issue-specific or corrective coaching typically has an identified starting goal.

The goal-setting conversation starts with the business issues and flows to leadership challenges and career-development aspirations. Some specific information on each of these three categories is already available from the selection interview. Often, this multi-lens perspective, albeit new, is easy for the executive to grasp. The opportunity for a more skillful intervention occurs when the executive is stuck. This could show itself as resistance to accepting the merit of including one or more of the three categories.

Addressing resistance without triggering defensiveness is a critical coaching skill. The coach's use of positional credibility to drive acceptance might elicit compliance, but it does not generate the commitment required to sustain change. It could also undermine the long-term relationship and further erode the coach's effectiveness. More significantly, that approach would miss the opportunity to more deeply understand the underlying values that are driving the resistant behaviors. Understanding those values is key to helping the executive determine whether they are still relevant and whether there are competing values that now hold more weight.

One client's boss was receiving organizational feedback that hinted at a potential career derailment. As I began working with this client, his discomfort with the idea of goals that concurrently touch all three areas was palpable. He was adamant that there should be only one type of goal and that was addressing the business issues in the best interest of the company—period. This resistance gave me the opportunity to explicate the underlying values. This executive had grown up in a military family with a lineage of high-ranking officers. The value set that permeated family conversations was always what was in the best interest of the country and the military branch. Personal interests were a far, far distant second. With this strong, disciplined family background around higher-level values and suppressed personal interests, he had come to work in a company that professed to hold those same values. As his career advanced, he became aware that the values espoused by an organization are not always the values that prevail in day-to-day operations.

Understanding the client's frame of reference can reveal the context of deeply held values and enable the coach to act from a place of empathetic attunement. With that attunement, the coach can discuss the value trade-offs the executive is making in the present context, in a way that is meaningful to the executive.

Another strategy for addressing resistance without triggering defensiveness is the use of stories and metaphors.[1] Stories do not take the place of having compelling logic and good systems thinking. Rather, stories open the pathway for those characteristics to shine through, making it easier for the executive to hear something new without creating a power struggle.

During a recent interview for a coaching assignment, it became obvious to me that the person who would benefit from coaching was the top executive, not the direct report he wanted me to work with and "fix." I committed to being authentic and began to share my thinking. I told him the story of my work with another relationship-conflict situation. In that case, the corporate executive turned to my client, the operating president, and said that he wanted to see the president work through the tough relationship issue his direct reports were embroiled in. The corporate executive explained his view that we do not always get the best stable of horses and, therefore, if the president expected to reach the next level, he needed to demonstrate capability in resolving relationship challenges. This completely shifted the thinking from "Why do I want to even mess with this?" to "This is an opportunity to figure out how to learn a critical career skill." Stories provide a non-confrontational way to invite thinking differently.

Most of the time, I do not have concerns that an executive is having a defensive reaction, and I simply share the logic and research behind the model. I start by sharing why I am looking for goals that overlap the three areas and provide a short example from team dynamics. I have used an example of the software design leader from a well-known high tech company who was singularly set on getting the microprocessor chip set designed for the exploding cell phone market by the commitment date. He had a great track record for hitting the chartered metrics, including commitment dates. And then things stalled out because no one wanted to work on his teams. He could not recruit people, which was how this firm typically built its teams. The members of his teams complained about not learning anything new and about being treated like fungible parts. They got burned out. He was operating his teams with only one goal in mind.

One of the leading thinkers and researchers on teams, J. Richard Hackman, says high-performing teams need three concurrent goals: (1) achieve the agreed-upon charter of the team, (2) develop capabilities to work more efficiently as a team, and (3) help team members grow their personal skill sets.[2] Hackman's view is grounded in much earlier work by Peter Drucker, who in *The Concept of the Corporation* observes, "It is typical of the most successful and the most durable institutions that they induce in their members an intellectual and moral growth beyond a man's original capacities."[3] From a systems perspective, the Seven-Stage Model has embedded the organization's needs, as well as the short-term leadership capability needs and the long-term career aspirations of the executive.

STAGE THREE: ENGAGE FEEDBACK SUPPORT TEAM

The early steps in this stage are straightforward. Working with the executive to select qualified participants and updating the goals into the interview protocol are clear-cut imperatives. The interview process requires some skill at teasing out usable examples, learning about the impact of behaviors, and managing time to keep the thirty-minute commitment.

Using a standardized interview protocol benefits everyone involved. The client benefits from knowing exactly what is going to be asked and how data is collected. The feedback participant, the person being interviewed, is put at ease as they are walked through a defined and well-articulated process. The coach asking the questions is guided by the process.

Five Common Challenges

In addition to the trial-and-error process of managing the time, there are five common challenges in the interview:

- Participants making sweeping generalizations
- The coach not asking for the business and emotional impact

- Participants pontificating on what the executive should do
- The coach addressing comments that may be excluded from the detailed reports
- The coach staying open and curious about cultural dimensions

Sweeping Generalizations

Many participants will start by answering with sweeping conclusions, "He is really good at that." That is an okay start and simply requires the coach to follow up with questions about the behaviors that led them to that conclusion. This technique of gaining the context and behavioral examples is easily learned. Corporate annual performance review processes offer this same advice to managers: to be specific and provide examples. Asking participants to link their conclusions back to observable behaviors is foundational. When the interviewer senses the participant jumping to a conclusion, the basic advice is to pause and ask what the participant saw the person do or say that led to that conclusion. The interview questions can be as simple as "What is an example that would make it easy for [the executive] to know what you are referring to?" I like this question as it is a gentle reminder that this process is in service to helping the executive. Other useful questions are "And what did she do that you found really helpful?" or "Is there anything else she did that has helped her make progress toward this goal?"

Not Asking for the Impact

The second challenge is for the coach to avoid assuming he knows the impact and neglecting to ask participants to describe what it was for them. A simple "What was the impact of that behavior?" suffices.

When I asked one participant, a new VP relating a restraining force, to describe the impact of the behavior, I heard a story that included a significant business impact, one the executive later admitted she had never considered. This question is neutral enough that it usually picks up both the business impact and the emotional impact, such as "I found myself losing trust." If the coach senses one of those impacts is not being addressed, additional questions may be needed.

Participant Pontification

The third interview challenge is the participant, the person being interviewed, who asserts having knowledge about what the executive should be doing and sees the interview as an opportunity to pontificate on these most excellent solutions. I state this with a bit of hyperbole to distinguish this behavior from the participant who slips in one or two solutions. With resolve, I maintain control of the interview process. I gently share that the purpose of the interview is to gather data that will help the executive decide where to focus and that we are not ready to move into generating solutions at this time. The idea is that this is not the time and it is not the participant's role or the purpose of this interview. A simple follow-up reminder is to restate the goal and get permission to proceed toward that goal. For example, "I would like to go back to exploring the behaviors that both drive and restrain [insert the specific goal]. Is that okay?"

Excluding Comments

The fourth challenge occurs when an issue surfaces in the interview that could be inflammatory or so sensitive that the person being interviewed may want to reconsider its inclusion. Repeating the request at the end of the conversation and asking for permission to share your detailed notes is ethically imperative. I flag comments during the interview and ask if they think this will be a problem. Usually those flagged comments are not a problem. The typical response I have heard is, "No, that is fine. He has heard it all before and it would be insincere not to include it here," or, "I said that to him in the hall yesterday and he needs to hear it officially." When there is a concern, whether picked up by an attuned coach or flagged by the interviewee, there are two ways to address it. The first is the obvious one of simply deleting the specific comment. The second is an offer to move the specific comment to a page I label as "anonymous feedback." There have been rare occasions when the person being interviewed requests that I include their comments only at the summary level and that I do not provide any detailed inputs from the interview.

Cultural Dimensions

The interviews are fast-moving dialogues on targeted goals. The questions are typically formulated in an organic manner, led by a healthy dose of curiosity. The people I interview often have different biases, cultural heritages, beliefs, values, experiences, and so on than I do. Being attuned to these possible differences can influence the coach's ability to make an authentic connection and use the flow of the conversation to inform the next question. David Clutterbuck suggests taking a pan-cultural lens, through which "we both value and are curious about how the world looks through difference, seeking greater awareness and understanding."[4] As the interviews are conducted via phone, differences most frequently show through language and choice of words or phrases. I try to keep my vocabulary geared toward achieving clear and unambiguous communication. Concurrently, I ask the person I am interviewing to say more whenever they use a word or phrase that is unusual or could have multiple meanings. In a recent feedback interview, the person I was interviewing used an expression that I thought I understood, but I was not quite sure I had it right. I asked for clarification of what she meant, and her explanation was more nuanced. When I was reviewing the feedback with my client, he appreciated the clarification.

Metabolizing the Feedback

The Seven-Stage Model is a feedback-intensive model that places emphasis on helping the client metabolize that feedback. The raw data of feedback has value only when the person receiving it integrates and metabolizes the new information into his existing schema or way of thinking. Preparing the client to receive feedback is one of the most challenging aspects of any coaching engagement, and may be even more so with the Stakeholder Feedback Interview methodology, because the feedback is so dense and specific.

At this point, the work of helping the client metabolize the feedback is four-fold:

- Organize the feedback for presentation to the executive
- Anticipate likely reactions when presenting the feedback
- Help the executive make sense of the data
- Invite the executive to immerse himself in the feedback with reflection

Organize the Feedback

Organizing the substantial amount of information gleaned from the interviews follows a three-step process. The first step is to transcribe the notes captured during the interviews. The second step is to identify the core ideas, both driving and restraining forces, for each participant. The third step is to synthesize those core ideas into larger themes and patterns.

The first step—transcription—is straightforward. The task during the interview is to capture the comments as closely as possible. While phone interviews make it easy to capture notes on a word processor, unless the interviewer is a great typist he'll need an amount of time equal to the time spent on the interview to correct the grammar, fill in what was not typed, and ensure readability. This is best done immediately after the interview to ensure freshness and accuracy. The format is provided by the interview protocol.

In the second step—identify core ideas—each idea from the interviews is converted into a pithy phrase. The direct reports for an executive supplied terms like this for one goal:

- Action guy: fire and then aim
- Stressed all the time
- Frenzy of activity
- Urgency the norm

There are many ways to cluster and group the transcriptions into summary themes. The one that works for me is to create another document. For each goal, I go through the driving forces, merging all the comments into one document. Then I do the same for the restraining forces, adding these comments to the same document. I continue this through all the goals and open-ended questions.

The third step—thematic clustering—further refines the data into the themes that really stand out. Preparing this in advance gives the coach the ability to move from the highest level to the core-idea summaries to the full-context comments from individuals.

I print the full document and begin by writing out a keyword or two in the margin next to each different comment and underline the salient words in the transcript. My final report will include the thematic clusters and a few bullets with the salient supporting comments as a summary section, followed by the complete transcript of each interview. The client receives this in both a PDF and a spiral-bound hard copy with tabs for each transcript.

The Stakeholder Feedback Interview Protocol is included in Appendix B. The Stakeholder Feedback Interview Report template can be found in Appendix C. Creating these documents is labor intense. The interviews are a full thirty minutes, and the process of transcribing my notes into something presentable to the client adds another thirty minutes each. Going from the individual transcripts to the summary report typically takes another three to four hours. For an interview process with eight interviewees, this is day and a half of time for the coach.

While that is a substantive amount of time, the result is highly informative to the client and guides the next steps in the Seven-Stage Roadmap. As noted earlier, the feedback data, backed up with specific observations, makes a compelling case that is difficult to dismiss or deny.

The goal is for the coach to enter the conversation with a well-organized package and enough familiarity with the interviews to enable him to support the themes with examples and anecdotes, as appropriate.

Anticipate Likely Reactions

If something strikes me during the interview as potentially disturbing, I ask the participant if the executive will already know this. More often than not, the answer is, "Yes, he has already heard this." That is great, as it signals a reduced risk of data that surprises or stings.

While the Seven-Stage Model embeds a process for gathering grounded feedback on the topics identified by the executive, the second task of preparing to give feedback recognizes that some of it can surprise and sting. As mentioned in the process description in Chapter 4, the coach starts the feedback process by reminding the client how much care and generosity the participants showed in responding. This is an important step, as there will be some natural anxiety about what will be in the report.

Some executives simply do not realize the impact of their behaviors on others. For a small minority of executives, the reaction can be especially hard to contain, because the behaviorally anchored observations from participants the executive chose are harder to dismiss with normal defense routines.

In one example, a relatively new executive found the results painfully disappointing. His reactions included anger and frustration. Like most of us, he did not expect to receive feedback that ran counter to his self-image (surprise) or that was unflattering (sting). Whenever emotions run in these directions, it is a good time to hit the pause button and talk with someone who can help you reflect and keep your perspective. This key function is served by a trusted and objective coach. The coach has to have the capacity to sit with someone in pain and discomfort without denying it, judging it, or wishing it away.

When this client dropped the reactivity, he could better see the magnitude of the gap between his well-intentioned actions and the not-so-well-received effect on others, and then he became curious and motivated. We talked through examples so that he could "see the system" and make sense of the reactions of his peers and direct reports. Making sense of both sides (his intent and the impact) was vital, as it enabled him to move from a "right-wrong" frame to an "unintended outcome" frame. In my work with this client, it was easy for him to say, "No, I was not trying to micromanage their efforts." With some candid discussions, he could also see exactly what he did that caused others to perceive his behaviors as micromanaging. This insight opened the door to new conversations.

Help Make Sense of the Data

The third step is to help the executive make sense of the feedback. The first cut through the process of making sense is to look for patterns and themes. There are always "one-off" comments and, while these may be tempting places to explore, the executive is best served by focusing on the areas where multiple participants provided similar feedback.

While the coach can help make sense of the data by linking back to individual stories and comments captured during the interviews, there is a limit to this approach. The coach models the patience of reflection by sitting with inputs that may not make sense to the executive, without either defending or dismissing the feedback. As always, these sticky spots create opportunities. In this case, that opportunity is for the executive to talk with the individual who provided the feedback and learn more about what was meant. The coaching task is to help the executive see the value of approaching this as building long-term relationships, where the gift of feedback is recognized and honored as a gift. With this mind-set, the executive enters the conversations with the feedback participants with appreciation and curiosity.[5] This attitude enables the conversations to become part of the work-group culture.

It would be wrong to make it sound as if this always goes smoothly. My most difficult example is an engagement in which I neglected to follow my own interview protocol and regretted it at the point of sharing the feedback. My client had asked that a higher-level executive in the organization be included as a feedback participant even though my client was not his direct report. Unfortunately, my best efforts did not result in behaviorally anchored feedback relevant to the specific goals that I would usually consider usable. The executive's feedback was extremely critical, with few balancing observations, but I decided to share it with the client because he had specifically asked for it. My client, a normally stoic male, was livid, hurt, angry, and dismissive.

To help the client gain some perspective and not take this feedback so personally, I asked him to analyze the comments and categorize them on a scale of how easy or hard it was to accept the feedback. If the feedback was congruent with his self-awareness, we placed it in the column labeled "nailed it." If the feedback was so discordant with his self-image that it generated a visceral "not me" response, we placed it in the column labeled "reject it." Those two anchor points were supplemented with middle columns labeled "work it" and "consider it."

My motivation for using the categorization technique was to clarify which items were his emotional land mines. He placed most of the executive's comments in the "reject it" column. My sense was that his overall emotional reaction caused him to shift items that he might otherwise have categorized in the middle two columns into the disowned category. Instead of helping my client become aware of his blind spots, previously given non-grounded and unbalanced feedback may have had the unintended consequence of rigidifying his blind spots. The client found justification for dismissing even the few comments that were supported by behavioral examples and placed them in the "reject it" column.

Invite Immersion and Reflection

Immersion and reflection are tightly interconnected with the third step; they are needed to build on the preliminary understanding. Appreciate the volume of material being handed to the executive. The tendency of almost all executives is to try to plow through this or any report as quickly as possible to glean the essential information. These feedback reports are not the dry reports executives are typically given. The reports are about their lives and carry an emotional valence.

I prepare executives to engage the material in a different, more intimate way. After helping them make sense of the data during our coaching conversation, I recommend that they read the report in depth when they are outside the hectic pace and interruptions of their work environment. And I hold them accountable to carve out this sacred time. Several clients have shared that they got a different perspective by asking their spouses to read the report and spending time together discussing it. What a beautiful way to invite our spouses into our lives in ways that add meaning and build connection.

I had a memorable experience of being introduced to new information in two different ways. I was going to attend a meditation retreat where one of the leaders had published a book that he would discuss during the retreat. Of course, in order to be prepared, I wanted to read it prior to the event, so I plowed through it in my standard fashion of learning something new with my left brain fully engaged. At the retreat, the author led us through exercises that activated the right side of our brains as he also introduced the concepts. My experience with grasping and integrating the concepts from this different state of mind was radically and pleasantly different.

STAGE FOUR: COMMIT TO ACTION

The feedback format lends itself well to developing action steps. There are normally sufficient driving forces, things the executive is doing that can get him to the goal. The work is usually focused on developing specific actions that address the most impactful restraining forces. Just because a change is obvious does not make it easy. That would be like saying losing weight has many favorable health and social benefits, so therefore it must be easy. An action plan that declares the equivalent of "Lose 10 pounds!" has the same likelihood of success as a New Year's resolution. The work in coaching is to use the shared understanding of context, values, and systemic issues to collaboratively create a fork in the road that leads to an alternative path.

I use a five-step process for recognizing the nature of the fork and for investigating the alternative paths:

1. Test for goal alignment. Ensure that the link between the goal and the targeted behavioral restraining force is clear.
2. Step outside the problem. Explore the problem with a broader perspective and context.
3. Reframe the problem. Stay vigilantly attentive to the right problem.
4. Define the other path. Collaborate to create robust action alternatives.

5. Create a learning context. Set up accelerated feedback loops through an action learning project.

Test for Goal Alignment

Ensure that the link between the goal and the targeted behavioral restraining force is clear.

This first step is a quick link back to the goal, making sure that both client and coach keep an eye on the higher-level goal they are trying to achieve. This goal-alignment check reaffirms the commitment to achieving results and gives the coach the authority to hold the executive accountable.

Step Outside the Problem

Explore the problem with a broader perspective and context.

Stepping outside the problem is a systems thinking tool that enables both the client and the coach to explore the issues with a broader perspective or context. While there are many techniques for exploring the interrelationships from a systems perspective, three techniques that prove especially helpful are: (1) checking for patterns of where the problem or restraining behaviors occur, (2) checking for patterns of the precipitating events or triggers, and (3) anticipating unintended consequences.

In the earlier example where I suggested that the higher-level executive was the one who needed coaching rather than his direct report, the tip-off that he was part of the problem and the solution came when I asked what had been done so far to address these issues. Coaching interventions had been made once before; things got better and then eroded again. From a systems perspective, when the driving forces of an outside intervention went away, the system reestablished equilibrium (homeostasis) at the old level. The intervention had targeted too narrow a piece of the larger system.

With a client with anger-management challenges, I was investigating for patterns of the triggers or precipitating events. I looked for clues about specificity with questions such as who was present, where did the undesirable behavior show up, and what were the surrounding circumstances. This significantly narrowed the scope of where special attention belonged. This technique provides the additional benefit of being able to build confidence by noting that since the client handles these situations well in one context, the basic underlying skill set is accessible and the work is to transfer existing skills into another context.

Unintended consequences are among the most common challenges. From a systems perspective, every change triggers unintended consequences. Sometimes they are simple misunderstandings, driven by the executive's approach or style. At other times, they are the results of lags or interdependencies that were not previously recognized. Whenever a client says, "Well, that was certainly not my intent," there is an opportunity to more fully understand the relevant elements within the system that have to be addressed to effect sustained change. With the examples from the Stakeholder Feedback Interviews as resource material, it is easy to look at specific situations.

Reframe the Problem

Stay vigilantly attentive to the right problem.

Testing for a possible way to reframe the problem flows naturally from the prior step of exploring the issues from a systems perspective. The coach benefits from the discipline of being constantly vigilant and holding a slight level of skepticism about whether she and the executive are working on the right goal and whether the goal is properly framed. Using the weight-loss metaphor, Weight Watchers strongly cautions against flash diets that quickly drop ten pounds, as all their research says that the weight will just come back. Similarly, executives can do the same thing in changing their behaviors for a short period of time. The standard of excellence for the Seven-Stage Model is sustained change through systemic change.

The level of investment one of my clients was displaying seemed low and completely out of proportion to the significance of the goals. I found myself with lots of self-doubts about how I might be getting in the way and what else I could be doing. Through my reflective work with my master coach, I realized that I was doing all of the heavy lifting. I brought the insight into the coaching conversation with the executive and we had a dialogue around the goals. The executive recognized that at an intuitive level, he knew we had not gotten the goals right. Once we went back to stepping outside the problem and reframing the problem, we found goals that provided the burst of energy that jumped the work to a higher level with exceptional outcomes.

Define the Other Path

Collaborate to create robust action alternatives.

With a high level of confidence that the right problem has been identified and framed within the correct level of the system, the next stage of work is to create viable options. The collaborative effort between the coach and the executive can usually develop robust alternative actions. There are numerous external resources that the coach can access to stir creative thinking, including (1) materials provided by the large coaching firms and organizations; (2) publications from leadership organizations, such as the Center for Creative Leadership and Harvard Business Publishing; and (3) a vast amount of literature available through online searches and bookstores.

The challenge is to comprehend why these ideas and viable options will work and why they might not work.

The following questions help check for value congruence, unintended consequences, manageability, and sufficiency:

- Have you explored the congruence between the new behaviors and your underlying values?
- Have you examined the potential unintended consequences of adopting these behaviors?
- Have you looked at your to-do list and assessed whether the action is manageable with everything else on your plate? Are these new tasks, or are they a new way of being in your leadership role?
- Have you convinced yourself that these actions are sufficiently robust to ensure achievement of your goal?

Create a Learning Context

Set up accelerated feedback loops through an action learning project.

The Seven-Stage Model is built on the concept that adult learners do best when three things are present: a challenging situation, feedback on progress, and a supportive environment. Action learning accelerates the change process by linking the coaching work to a specific application in the workplace, which provides a manageable context for the executive to practice as well as coaching support to capture the learnings.[6]

Over the years, I have monitored the results of my coaching engagements with an eye to what activities make a difference. Action learning projects stand out as being correlated with the most successful engagements. These projects are simply specific contexts in which the new behavior is applied. For one client, the action learning project was to practice his targeted behaviors around building effective teams in his role as lead for a multinational team that had a six-month charter. For another client, the action learning project was to work on her goal of running effective meetings in her role at the monthly cross-departmental operations reviews. Simple technique, powerful results.

STAGE FIVE: MEASURE SUCCESS

In the Seven-Stage Model, measuring success is recommended during the coaching engagement and near the end of the engagement. During the engagement, feedback plays a new role in gauging the efficacy of the changes the executive has made. This accelerated feedback loop matters, as it can be a frustratingly long time before others notice that you are doing something differently. Often they sense something is different, like a new haircut, but cannot quite figure out what it is. In order to accelerate the positive feedback loops, clients are encouraged to actively seek feedback on how they are doing. For example, with a client who was working to overcome anxiety at giving presentations, we developed a feedback form that she then gave to a few confidants who attended her presentations and agreed to provide her with feedback. For another client, a subset of the participants in his Stakeholder

Feedback Interview have been regularly approached to give feedback on what they are observing. In this case, one person gave material feedback when she said, "I heard you talking about that, but I have not yet seen you do it." This was a nice reminder that the performance standard is the change in behavior, not the intention to do it.

Near the end of an engagement, I ask an executive to gather feedback from a subset of the same participants in the Stakeholder Feedback Interview. The client is asked to take leadership of the Mini–Stakeholder Interview process. Refer to Appendix E. Of course, this is not a completely foreign task, as the executives have been given small assignments to gather specific feedback throughout the coaching engagement. Likewise, the coach has been gathering feedback from the executive on the results of the behavioral changes identified in the action plan throughout the engagement.

If the client has reservations about conducting these goal-focused interviews, I invite an exploration of what is getting in the way, the restraining forces. This approach typically yields important insights into the reluctance some executives have to seeking targeted feedback.

I have experimented with three approaches to conducting the Mini–Stakeholder Interview: one in which the client does the interviews, another in which the coach conducts the interviews, and a third in which the Mini–Stakeholder Interview is sent via Survey Monkey. My strong preference is the client-conducted option. Having the executive conduct these feedback interviews has the practical benefit of creating comfort with a powerful technique for getting direct feedback, which exponentially increases the chances that they will use this technique in the future.

After the coach and client review the results of the Mini–Stakeholder Interview, the coach integrates that information into a Final Coaching Report (see Appendix E). This report is given to the client. The client has the option of sharing it with his manager as part of the three-way meeting in the Sustain Progress stage. This report documents key elements of progress and introduces any leading-edge issues. For each participant in the stakeholder interviews, a complete transcript of the conversation is appended as a separate section of the report.

STAGE SIX: SUSTAIN PROGRESS

As noted earlier, the deliverable from this stage is a closure conversation with the executive and his sponsor. This meeting provides a high-level overview of progress made and builds in ongoing support from the sponsor. The executive has the opportunity to share facets of the pre and post information gathered.

These meetings tend to flow well. The client's boss knows through the invitation that the purpose of the meeting is to review the results of the coaching and discuss how the boss can be supportive in sustaining the changes. The confidentiality roles were established months ago; the coach can talk to the process issues (level of engagement, doing the hard work, etc.), and the client can share the content specifics.

These meetings create small opportunities to reinforce elements of the Seven-Stage Model. The first opportunity occurs when the conversation turns into a glowing congratulatory meeting, complete with sweeping platitudes. While these can be highly complimentary and nice to hear, the point is that usable feedback is specific and behaviorally anchored. With humor and a nod to the coaching process, I will ask the client's boss for an example of what she has seen that led her to that nice-to-hear conclusion. Then I will reinforce those behaviors by noting how or why that was helpful. The second opportunity is when the client's boss wants to immediately change to the next issue, rather than talk about providing ongoing support. Because every now and then the boss does not know what to do to provide ongoing support, in advance of the meeting I ask the client what support he would like his boss to provide. These ideas can be used to prime the pump and start the conversation.

STAGE SEVEN: PROVIDE FEEDBACK TO COACH

The deliverable from this stage of the Seven-Stage Model is a feedback report on the coach (see Appendix D). While some clients prefer to complete this feedback report in advance and in writing, others prefer to complete it through conversation.

The coach has the transformational opportunity to use this information in the service of enhancing his level of practice. The challenge is attitudinal. Are we willing to ask for feedback on the topics most dear to us? Are we willing to admit the imperfections of our models, of our knowledge, or of our interventions in service to improving and growing? Are we willing to give of ourselves fully and place our leadership authority in the service of helping other leaders, the executives we coach?

The approach to metabolizing this feedback is the same as the approach described above for the executive. The only difference is that the conversations are taking place with a master coach. I find it both satisfying and humbling to be holding myself to the same standard and process to which I hold my clients.

Chapter Seven

Getting the Support and Reflection Coaches Need

The earlier chapters in this book relate to the executive coach's skills and processes. This chapter adds depth by focusing on the importance of continuous learning to coaching work.

This chapter offers four pathways for getting support and addresses three questions for reflection:

1. Are the actions and initiatives we are pursuing sufficient to support our ongoing growth and learning needs?
2. How do we discover those areas in which we would benefit from more insight? What are the early warning signals?
3. What are the barriers to getting the ongoing feedback we need to grow and learn?

QUESTIONS FOR REFLECTION

1. Are the actions and initiatives we are pursuing sufficient to support our ongoing growth and learning needs?

We benefit from challenging ourselves, whether as a new or a well-tenured coach, by asking this question. There is recognition, especially in Europe, that coaches and clients both derive benefits from the coach being in some form of relationship that provides ongoing feedback and opportunities for reflection. In the United States, this recognition is increasing at a much slower pace. However, there has been significant growth in the number of executive coaches participating in coaching supervision programs.[1] While pursuing continuing education units or certifications certainly has value, the ongoing nature of feedback and reflection, whether with a colleague, a group, a mentor, or a supervisor, can be a key practice differentiator. My experience is that coaches optimize their effectiveness by being in any of these ongoing professional relationships.

While in the role of coordinator for leadership development for AMD's Austin campus, I was responsible for assessing developmental needs and delivering leadership training programs to address those needs. I thought I was pretty good at it. Then I asked some of the participants for feedback on a course I taught. They looked at me with a vague, distant expression and asked me to give them a hint as to what we had covered. Ouch! I started designing-in action learning concepts,[2] geared toward ensuring that the participants had the opportunity to rehearse and then practice what was being taught. That worked better than my simple class role-plays, but then the feedback was that they did not know how to adapt the class material to their real-world situation. My next modification was adding coaching sessions to support the iterations essential for adult learning. This worked so well that it anchored my decision to become a leadership consultant and executive coach. The benefits of working in a rich feedback environment, one built on positive relationships and candid dialogue, provided a pivotal difference in the effective transfer of knowledge from a classroom to the work context.

Adult learning theory suggests that learning is enhanced by internal motivation.[3] Motivations for coaches to expand their own feedback environment may vary widely, including:

- Building skills and capabilities
- Driving better outcomes for the client
- Feeling wholeness and purpose[4]
- Seeking greater presence[5]
- Overcoming feeling stuck
- Earning advanced certification
- Enhancing personal and professional confidence
- Recognizing our own barriers to change
- Realizing our potential

Even with the best of motivations for creating their own feedback and reflection environment, coaches may not be as successful at getting the feedback they need to make progress. At the highest level, coaching is about helping the client change behaviors. We work with our clients to clarify and define the problem area, locate that problem in their work context, cocreate possible solutions, develop action plans to implement the solutions, evaluate the outcomes, and design-in support for continued success. We can do the same work for ourselves.

2. How do we discover those areas where we would benefit from more insight? What are the early warning signs?

In my own coaching work, there always seem to be a few rough spots where a bigger toolkit or more reflection would prove helpful. As coaches, we are constantly making judgments on how to interpret information: when to ask for specific examples, when to push back, when to offer feedback, when to share how we are feeling, when to reframe the issue, and so on. There is never a shortage of challenges that would benefit from more growth and knowledge!

Supervision is one of the pathways to getting support. The definition of *supervision* used in this chapter follows that of the European Mentoring and Coaching Council (EMCC) Global: "a safe space for reflective dialogue with a practicing supervisor, supporting the supervisee's practice, development and well-being."[6]

Peter Hawkins developed the seven-eyed process model of supervision (see Figure 4).[7] This model derives its name by looking at the coaching engagement through seven different lenses. The first four lenses are the most relevant for identifying early warning signals that could serve as the motivation for seeking ongoing feedback. The last three lenses are related to the feedback environment that has been cocreated and how that can be used to stimulate further learning and growth. While I have identified a robust sample of these early warning signals based on my coaching experiences, coaches will have a unique list based on their experiences. Identifying and articulating these in the context of current cases is one of the primary benefits of seeking ongoing feedback.

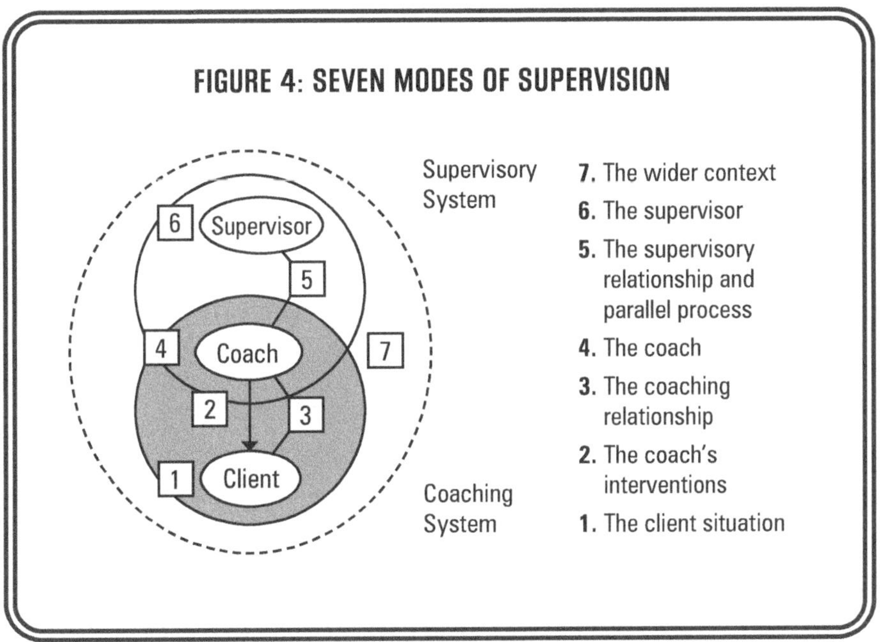

Source: Adapted from P. Hawkins and E. Turner, *Systemic Coaching: Delivering Value Beyond the Individual*, New York: Routledge, 2019, p. 153.

The Client Situation Lens

Here the focus is on how the coach understands the client and how they present, as well as the relationship between the client and the organization.

- *Missed something.* In one case, as I reviewed my notes, I discovered that I didn't probe enough about the client's work context to fully understand and appreciate how serious the issue was that she was presenting. My motivation to seek feedback is often driven by curiosity about what I was missing that would give me a more congruent picture of the client's world.

- *Cultural barriers*. Awareness of the culture and broader organizational context is an important source of data. Knowing how the organization's values and assumptions affect the client can provide insight into what options are viable. Perhaps more importantly, increasing the clients' awareness of these may help them realize it is not so personal or not just about them. These are sometimes hard to see—the phrase "fish don't see the water" comes to mind—which is exactly why we may benefit from working with a trusted third party or colleague.

The Coach's Interventions Lens

The focus here is on strategies and interventions used by the coach.

- *Too sure of myself.* The father of modern social psychology, Kurt Lewin, is often quoted as saying, "There is nothing more practical than a good theory."[8] Early in my career, I would often feel quite certain I had it all figured out and forget about suspending judgment and framing the issues as a good theory or a working hypothesis. Now, I use the sense of righteous certainty as a clarion bell that something is amiss, and I seek out the inputs from a trusted colleague. My supervisor and I have explored questions such as "Why was I so absolutely certain?" and "Where else have I gotten in trouble doing this?" and "What else is keeping me from forming alternative, viable hypotheses?" Tough questions with some great learning!

- *Not sure of myself.* At the other end of the spectrum, there have been times when I felt uncertain about what to do next. My interventions were not proving helpful. Many times, this can be addressed by reviewing my notes and giving myself the gift of more reflection time. Other times, I found that a more efficient process was exploration with a colleague. Issues we discussed included conversations about gaps in our cocreation process. For example, was I letting the client off the hook and taking on a role that was more comfortable for the client but had the unintended consequence of creating an imbalance in how we were holding each other accountable?
- *Understanding their pickle.* Clients get themselves caught in dilemmas in which their interests and intents do not align. Sometimes identifying these are straightforward and easy. At other times, we have both found ourselves stumbling around and missing the core dilemma. Whenever I felt like we were incorrectly framing the core dilemma, it also felt like the interventions we created were off the mark or less potent and impactful. Just as we help our clients frame and reframe their issues, coaches can benefit from a neutral and trusted colleague helping us do this. In relationship with my supervisor, I was able to understand how I was not proactive enough in exploring the client's constraints to change. Since then, I've so internalized that concept that I added a worksheet to help surface the constraints (see Appendix A).

The Client-Coach Relationship Lens

The focus is on the system and relationship that the client and coach have cocreated.

- *Self-management skills.* Chapter 5 describes core self-management skills for building the relationship between the coach and the client. Those primary skills include attuned empathy, self-awareness, self-compassion, authenticity, and multiple roles. When any of these are missing, the quality of the relationship will be affected. Other self-management skills that can lead to a poor relationship and the consequent increase in risk-avoidant behaviors include intolerance of ambiguity, rushing to closure on a goal, or taking on an expert role. The challenge with self-management skills is that we are most often not the best judge, which is why a trusted other can be so helpful.
- *Too much in the system.* A technique used in qualitative research is to hold a participant-observer stance, in which you are both a participant and can stand outside the system looking in with an objective observer perspective. Losing that objectivity has had lots of implications on my work, including my willingness to push or to support the client. Seeking external feedback can help restore our participant-observer balance. A trusted colleague can ask grounding questions, with an invitation to look at the situation from above it and with less emotional engagement. I find this form of framing to be helpful in regaining my ability to see the whole system in context.

- *Relationship issues.* There are clients I enjoy spending time with, marked by an easy repartee and free-flowing conversations. And there are clients with whom that is not the case. Addressing these client-coach interface issues with a trusted colleague has been effective in addressing my issues. The trusted colleague I sought out for a consult pushed me to a deeper level of self-awareness with questions such as "What exactly is causing this reaction in you?" and "What is the impact of not sharing that with your client?" While I struggled to answer these questions, that was exactly what I needed to do.

The Coach Lens

The focus is on the coach and what is being stimulated or triggered by the engagement.

- *What keeps me up.* When I find the same unresolved issue intruding into my consciousness, without a clear plan for resolution, it is a strong signal that I do not yet have the internal resources to fully understand or explore the issue. There are so many moving parts that underlie these issues that I want to bounce those against a trusted colleague before bringing my concerns and insights into the client space. That can feel like having a friend help me untangle a Gordian knot.
- *My emotions.* As coaches, we are not expected to be unemotional others to be used as the client's self-object. In fact, quite the opposite is true if we are to be in an authen-

tic relationship. Clients will stir things up in me that, if left unattended, could preclude me from being fully present with them. Yvonne Agazarian, founder of the Systems-Centered Training and Research Institute, always asked what was going on in our bodies on the belief that our bodies knew before our brains did.[9] I found this somatic attunement to be sage advice. Physiological signs indicate an area that would benefit from further work. And I find that years after her training, I still miss some of my signs (e.g., foot tapping, teeth grinding, tummy tightening). The good news is that the trusted colleagues I have used over the years for feedback are good at spotting these.

- *Here and now.* The warning that I may need to gain more personal awareness occurs when I find myself self-censoring rather than bringing my experiences into the room in a nonjudgmental way. The client loses potentially valuable insights when I close off aspects of how I am feeling. An example is when I found myself getting more agitated and impatient and did not bring that up but rather acted out on it. This links directly to the example above on attunement to how my body was reacting. One of my supervisors, with the softest of hands, asked me when I had given up on my client's ability to think himself out of his dilemma. Even with soft hands, there was a sting to the comment. However, the ensuing conversation led to a set of very constructive insights and interventions.
- *Blind spots.* This is the great unknown. Sometimes I'll find myself with a hint that something is amiss. It is as if the

issue is right around the corner, and I just cannot see it. A recent example was with a client who was trying to face his fears. Without even thinking about it, I dropped his signal that this emotion was important to him. It was only with the feedback from a trusted colleague that I gained an understanding of how important this may be for the client and insight into why I was avoiding his invitation to explore this feeling. My own experience and that of many coaches I know is that we find deep satisfaction when we can authentically attune and be present with our clients across a broadening range of issues, emotions, and challenges.

- *Digging around.* Reflecting on each coaching case and identifying two or three areas where I have curiosity about how to improve is a solid discovery technique. It is as if those nuggets are always there, just waiting to be discovered! The act of taking time to reflect on the case from an observer perspective almost always opens areas for further exploration.

3. What are the barriers to getting the ongoing feedback we need to grow and learn?

With so many benefits to engaging with a trusted other to cocreate a feedback environment, one should pause and explore the barriers to getting the feedback we need to grow and learn. As Agazarian points out, it is typically more efficient to address the barriers than to keep pushing on the driving forces.

- *Relationship matters.* It is difficult to find the person or group with whom we can develop an authentic and non-defended relationship. As detailed in the earlier section on the Hierarchy of Change, the relationship between the person giving the feedback and the person receiving the feedback has a strong influence on the quality and usefulness of the information offered as well as on the receptivity to that information. Sometimes we do not give ourselves the gift of time and familiarity that are important to deepening the openness of the relationship.

- *Risk-taking requirement.* The two-way street of feedback is plagued by risks on both sides. It is precisely these risks that make developing safety and trust in relationship so imperative. Colleagues and coaches willing to provide candid feedback make themselves vulnerable to creating ill will, to having their ego bruised, to having to let go of outdated thinking, and so on. Personal experience and the research in the feedback field is replete with cautions on the risks of giving feedback.[10]
- *Self-exposure.* On the receiving side, coaches and colleagues asking for feedback take the risk of disclosing goals that are especially salient to their success or of exposing areas they perceive to be weaknesses. They also risk being judged as uncertain or insecure. Ironically, while this risk may keep us from seeking feedback, the reality is that exposing oneself by seeking feedback that might be negative improves constituents' opinion of that person's overall effectiveness.[11]
- *Long view.* As it was for Dr. Atul Gawande, who sought feedback when he was already an accomplished surgeon,[12]

continual improvement requires taking a long view. This lifelong learner approach anchors the continuous professional development model advocated by Peter Hawkins and Nick Smith.[13] Taking a long-term perspective also requires a steadfast commitment to continuous improvement. If this were easy, professional organizations, in any field, would not dedicate so much effort to continuing education certification requirements.

- *Too costly.* There are lots of conversations among supervisors who are certified and seeking to expand their practice about what rates they should charge. The recent "Global Coaching Supervision" report revealed that about two-thirds of supervisors charged between $100 and $300 per session.[14] Of course, working in a group context reduces the per-session cost substantially. In my own coaching practice, I have been embedding the cost of being supervised in the fees I charge the client. I am explicit in my contracting that I will be receiving supervision, framing that as a value-add. Building a coaching practice and sustaining economic viability can be challenging. Providing a high level of service to our clients is also a challenge. Finding the right balance across this apparent dilemma is important and up to the individual to decide. As my supervisor once asked me, "Have you considered the cost of not doing . . . ?"

PATHWAYS TO BUILDING A RESOURCE SYSTEM

So far, this chapter has been about the motivations for entering into an ongoing feedback relationship and some of the challenges or barriers you may have to address before entering such a relationship. Now, I address how to get the support and offer four pathways to building a resourcing system.

Colleagues

One pathway is through networking opportunities, such as International Coaching Federation (ICF) chapter meetings, coaching events, or voluntary coaching opportunities, in which you have the chance to interact with and get to know other coaches. A similar benefit can be found through organizations such as the Center for Creative Leadership, where the coaches have periodic information-sharing sessions. The idea is to go into "scan mode" in search of kindred spirits for both personal and professional growth. Having a favorable personal relationship is a great entre to building a professional relationship. These collegial relationships can evolve into regular dyadic meetings to discuss the challenges both parties face in their coaching work.

Groups

Working in a group context can be an affordable and beneficial way to get support and expand your thinking. It is also a great way to broaden your network. Groups with a shared goal have a wonderful ability to adapt and make space across a wide range of individual styles, personalities, leadership, and processes. Julie Hays provides four benefits derived from working in a group: learning from overseeing the supervision of others, realizing we share the same issues, moving beyond shame and reframing mistakes as learning opportunities, and monitoring ourselves for triggers.[15] To her list I would add that groups provide a good place to sharpen our skills at reflective thinking[16] and that groups are more affordable and therefore likely more sustainable. I have been actively involved with three different group approaches. The first was formed on the Master Mind concept,[17] tailored for coaches. We agreed on a collective goal that permitted any coaching-related issue and that each group would be guided by a trained facilitator. One's experience or levels of coaching certification were not factors in admission to the group. An experienced facilitator was assigned to balance the open-admission criteria. The second group also shared a common goal, but one quite different from the first group. The shared goal was to gain insights about a current coaching case. This was a group of peers who had completed their coaching supervision training together and was guided by a certified coaching supervisor acting as facilitator. The third approach differs from the first two in that it is peer-led, working in dyads with a goal of building our skills as supervisors. This is a long-term ongoing group, in which the trust, safety, and relationships continue to deepen. Additional details on these three group processes are included in Appendix F.

Mentor

Enlist the mentoring services of someone who has the necessary training and skills that you are seeking. ICF mentor coaches are a great resource, as they have been certified at focusing their knowledge, skills, and experience within the context of coaching competencies.

Supervisor

The last resource is hiring a coach who has completed a coaching supervision program. The role of the supervisor is different from that of the mentor. Whereas the domain of knowledge for the mentor is anchored by the coaching competencies, the knowledge domain of the supervisor is more holistic and systemic.[18]

While there are other approaches that a coach can take to create the feedback environment for reflective thinking, it is important to create your own feedback environment. As noted in Chapter 2, the neurophysiology research has determined that we assess for safety before we selectively turn off our defenses. This aligns with my own experience coaching, supervising coaches, and being supervised. When we establish relationships marked by high levels of safety and trust, we are more likely to replace defensive routines with openness, curiosity, and a willingness to think reflectively. Relationships matter because they expand the feedback environment, which enables others to take the risks of being vulnerable and sharing information that might be hard to hear.

Each of the above four approaches can have powerful takeaways, moving from establishing safety and trust, to building relationships, to enhancing the feedback environment, to seeing issues from a systems perspective, to building resources for sustaining change. Not coincidentally, these are exactly the stages identified in the Hierarchy of Sustained Change detailed in Chapter 2. This chapter applies the principles in the earlier chapters of this book to the coach. As a relationship with a trusted other supports the work of growth and change for clients, it equally applies to coaches. This chapter focuses on the importance of continuous learning for professional growth, challenging ourselves to know if we are doing enough, and identifying potential barriers to getting ongoing feedback and support. The chapter concludes with suggestions on various pathways to expanding resource systems for attaining that continuous learning. The emphasis is on developing relationships with trusted others, which enables the feedback and reflection necessary to support growth and development as coaches.

Chapter Eight

Exploring Professional Ethical Dilemmas

This chapter explores the ethical dilemmas inherent in coaching and provides a process for addressing those dilemmas. A recent study conducted by EMCC revealed that over 70% of coaches face between one and four ethical professional dilemmas per year.[1] As Donald Schön put it almost forty years ago, "Practitioners are frequently embroiled in conflicts of values, goals, purposes, and interests."[2] There are many definitions of an ethical dilemma.[3] The working definition of an ethical dilemma used in this chapter includes the following elements: (1) the need to make a difficult choice or decision (2) between two or more courses of action, (3) all of which are unsatisfactory, (4) as the choices do not comply with ethical norms.

As coaches we benefit from awareness of ethical norms from multiple perspectives. We have our personal ethical values, our profession's ethical standards of behavior, and the ethical expectations of the organization that is funding our coaching services. The various professional associations for coaching have attempted to codify ethical behavior on the part of their members. The dominant coaching association in the United States, the International Coaching Federation (ICF), identifies twenty-eight separate ethical standards.[4] Other coaching and mentoring organizations have made important strides toward developing a unified global code of ethics.[5] And yet, as specific as the efforts of these various professional organizations have been at explicating ethical behaviors, Ioanna Iordanou, Rachel Hawley, and Christiana Iordanou note in *Values and Ethics in Coaching* that "no unified code of ethics can alleviate the challenges of making ethical decisions."[6]

Increasing one's pool of explicit knowledge by learning the ethical core values and standards of our profession is a necessary but insufficient step in addressing the challenges of making ethical decisions. The conversion of our tacit or implicit knowledge of our ethical values is missing. Tacit knowledge is knowledge that is difficult to express or extract, like playing a musical instrument or driving a car. While explicit knowledge is reflected in our ethical standards and codes of conduct, tacit knowledge is rooted in our context, experience, practices, and values. It is made explicit through reflective practices such as mentoring, shadow coaching, and supervision.[7] Supplementing the core ethical values and standards of our profession with both an ethical decision-making model and a relationship with a coaching supervisor provides more-robust solutions and supports the coach in expanding what psychologist James Rest refers to as one's moral sensitivity and judgment.[8]

The RFDA model introduced in this chapter is designed to support the reflective practice of the coach and thus expand the conversion of tacit to explicit knowledge. As indicated by the examples in Chapter 7, the process of learning through reflection is greatly increased when we reflect-in-relationship—that is, when we have a qualified trusted other to help us move past our normal defensive routines and fully address the ethical challenges we face. Adding a structured approach for making ethical decisions supplements and deepens those conversations. When we make explicit the judgments about which action is right, we are adding clarity and depth to our personal code of ethics. Similarly, when we make explicit how we are interpreting a particular situation, forming alternatives about how to behave, and assessing the impact of our choices, we are adding clarity to our personal code of ethics.

RFDA MODEL FOR ETHICAL DECISION MAKING

This chapter introduces an ethical decision-making model and applies that model to a range of case situations. A colleague and I developed the RFDA (recognize, frame, diagnose, act) model to help our graduate students in a master's program in organizational leadership and ethics address the challenges faced in making ethical decisions and to build their internal awareness of the value system they were using to guide their decisions.[9] This is a four-stage model that includes, as the acronym suggests, recognizing, framing, diagnosing, and acting. The model integrates three bodies of knowledge: the works of adult learning theorists who stress the role of learning in-action through reflection,[10] the works of ethicists who advocate that ethics requires a reflective process built on reason and choice,[11] and the view of business academics that knowledge is primarily tacit and benefits from being made explicit through reflection. The unifying thread through these bodies of knowledge is the focus on the potency of reflection to learn from our experiences. This chapter extends that thinking to add the importance of being in-relationship for support as we use reflection to address current ethical challenges and to deepen our ethical sensitivity and judgment.

Recognize

The first stage is to consciously recognize that there is an ethical dilemma. This RFDA stage requires explication of tacit knowledge by answering "What led you to conclude that this was an ethical issue?" Questions that may prove helpful include:

- What are you paying attention to (your early detection system)?
- What is your body telling you (somatic symptoms)?
- What did you see and observe?
- What facts do you know and not know?
- Who are the stakeholders involved, or who could be touched by this?
- What are you curious about?

Frame

The second RFDA stage is to frame the ethical concerns and observations within a conceptual context. This moves the coach from a tacit level of awareness to one that is more explicit and can be discussed. This stage also requires understanding of the values and beliefs both the coach and the client bring to the situation. Our graduate students found it challenging to write a one-page document detailing their personal concept of ethical leadership, which is why working in relationship with another is so valuable in teasing out espoused values. While it is not necessary to have read ethicists such as Kant, Bentham, Rawls, or Aristotle, most coaches have a reasonable grounding in the following ethical concepts or know how to quickly access this information online. The following ethical approaches include a short concept statement followed by relevant passages from the ICF Code of Ethics.[12]

- *Most good:* This involves doing what creates the most good. "I adhere to the philosophy of 'doing good' versus 'avoiding bad.'"
- *Rules:* Rules are expressed clearly and should be followed. "Maintain the strictest levels of confidentiality. . . . As an ICF Professional, . . . I acknowledge and agree to fulfill my ethical and legal obligations to my coaching Client(s), Sponsor(s), colleagues and to the public at large."
- *Justice:* Everyone is treated equally. "Avoid discrimination by maintaining fairness and equality in all activities and operations, while respecting local rules and cultural practices."
- *Rights:* This approach respects individual rights. "Create an agreement/contract regarding the roles, responsibilities and rights of all parties involved. . . . Have a clear understanding about how information is exchanged. . . . Respect all parties' right to terminate."
- *Virtue:* A person's actions are morally consistent with the kind of person they want to be—honest, brave, just, gener-

ous, and so on. "Recognize and honor the contributions and intellectual property of others. . . . [I am] honest and work within recognized scientific standards . . . when conducting and reporting research."

- *Common good:* This involves having high expectations for overall good. "Commit to excellence through continued personal, professional and ethical development."

The following questions presume a growing awareness of our internal value system and of the various ethical approaches. Questions that may prove helpful with framing include:

- Which of the above ethical approaches could help you make sense of your experience?
- How could a specific ethical approach be applied to this situation?
- What other approaches or codes of conduct could work?
- What additional data or context is needed to apply a specific ethical framework?
- How do your assumptions and attributions shape what you saw?
- Who could you talk with to gain more insight on these questions?

Diagnose

In the third stage, the coach articulates options and assesses the outcomes of any potential actions. Consideration is given to both intended and unintended consequences and to possible individual, organizational, and systemic outcomes. Too frequently, everyone jumps on their first choice without thinking systemically about all the stakeholders, options, and consequences. Further, coaches may not even be aware of the various available resources (ethical hotlines, ethical codes, internal values, colleagues, coaching supervisor). The outcome of this stage is conscious discernment of options and the possible impact of those options. Questions that have proven helpful include:

- What are the resources available to help me figure out my options?
- What are the potential outcomes for each stakeholder group with each option?
- What arc thc possible unintended consequences, both short term and long term?
- Is there alignment between these actions and my personal values and beliefs?
- Where there is a lack of alignment, what could be causing that?

Act

Through the implementation of this model, one moves from being a casual observer to being a sophisticated gatherer, interpreter, and diagnostician of ethical behavior. The fourth stage, act, is the culmination or synthesis of the prior stages as concrete actions are identified. At this stage, the coach has the opportunity to validate and authenticate personal philosophy and deeply held beliefs. A specific course of action is decided. To reiterate the challenge of an ethical dilemma, any choice made will not be completely satisfying. The best antidote to avoiding unethical behavior is being mindful of context and choices.[13] Questions that assist thinking in the act stage include:

- What am I specifically committed to do?
- With whom will I share this decision either before or after I act?
- Is there a timing component to implementing this decision?
- Is there a need for documentation with this action?
- What parts of my belief system are reinforced by this decision?
- What values or beliefs do I need to change because of this experience?
- What have I learned?

CASE EXAMPLES

Confidentiality and the Organization Example

I was considering working as a coach in a new organization, one with which I was not familiar. The head of their human resources and organizational development (HROD) department shared that their organization required a final written report that documented the goals and outcomes from the coaching engagement as a standard practice.

Recognize

As I felt my stomach tighten but could not quite articulate the source of my uneasiness, I suspected there was an ethical issue. I knew myself well enough to know something did not feel right. Did I have the information and context I needed? Is this an organization in which the norms include this type of reporting? Was I overreacting because I've seen written reports misused elsewhere? I felt myself being flooded with questions! I shared with the HROD person that this requirement was new to me and that I wanted to think it over and get back to her.

Frame

While the first stage of the RFDA model helped me recognize that I needed to think more deeply, the second stage provided conceptual context. Do the executives support this level of disclosure or nonconfidentiality? Do the people I will be coaching (junior executives being groomed for higher-level roles) buy in to this requirement? I sought out the executive who introduced me to the organization, and he explained that this level of transparency is exactly what the organization felt made their company so successful. In turn, he introduced me to several junior executives who had recently gone through this executive development program. They explained how typical receiving written feedback was and that everyone in this executive development program trusted that senior leadership had their best interests at heart, and they readily agreed to the written reports from the coach. It became abundantly clear that this type of candor and openness was a core part of this organization's culture. Even though everyone in the organization consistently expressed a desire for transparency, I did not think that fully absolved me of my obligations as a coach. I used the above list of ethical approaches and the support of a trusted colleague to help me think this through.

Most good: While everyone in the organization seemed to think their ethical approach created the most good, I was not sure. It wasn't until a conversation with my colleague that we surfaced an important element of my personal value system: I did not believe I was the best-qualified person to judge the success of the coaching engagement.

Rules: There are confidentiality rules in the ICF Code of Ethics, and there are guidelines on potential conflicts of interests between the client and the sponsoring organization. Even though the potential clients seemed fine with the current arrangement, I was not sure if I would be recruited as a substitute for direct communication between the client and the organization (triangulation) or caught in a bind somewhere downstream.

Justice: All the coaches hired for this executive development program followed the same protocol of submitting a final report detailing the goals and outcomes for each of the participants.

Rights: While there was a detailed contract of services between the coaches and the organization, there was some fuzziness about how the final report would be used. Would this report be used by HROD to evaluate the coach/coaching program? Would it be used in future performance evaluations conducted by operational executives? At the same time, I recognized that the organization had the right to ensure the coaching was delivering the desired results. There was also an issue of my own boundary management around confidentiality. While I do not feel I have the right to share content issues a client discusses in our coaching sessions, I was in a quandary because the clients in this organization were fine with my sharing.

Virtue: Would I be required to submit potentially career-damaging reports, and would I be okay with myself if I did that? I was in a bind. First, I view my role as a coach as being supportive and developmental, not judgmental and evaluative. Second, as mentioned earlier, I do not believe a coach is in the best position to evaluate the effectiveness of a coaching engagement. Conducting myself as if I were in the best position to do that would not be consistent with the kind of coach I want to be.

Common good: The organization had been running this executive development program with a significant coaching element in this way for years. All parties involved felt they had a programmatic process that delivered positive results. There were no complaints or contrary indicators.

I recognized that how I framed the issues would cause me some internal tension and would likely cause me to expand or modify my personal values and beliefs. I did not want to be one of those coaches David Clutterbuck described when he wrote about how coaches can fail to challenge their own self-narratives.[14] I certainly got what I asked for. Upon reflection, with support from my colleague, we identified three sticking points: (1) most good—I did not believe the coach was best qualified to judge the success of the coaching engagement, (2) rights—my internal beliefs about confidentiality were in conflict with the organization's rights to evaluate the engagement, and (3) virtue—would I be required to submit potentially career-damaging reports, and would I be okay with myself if I did that?

Diagnose

The first two stages of RFDA gave me better information and a framework for deeply thinking about how I should respond. The diagnose stage is about identifying the alternatives and evaluating the consequences of any action or inaction. I started with the two obvious choices: option 1, to accept the engagement and be as conscientious as possible in writing the end report, or option 2, to decide not to work for this organization. Were there other options that could alleviate the challenges unearthed in the last stage?

While this could turn into a lucrative engagement, I wanted to hold that thought aside, as the money was not the most pressing question. I could not fully absolve myself of my obligations as a coach. How could I mitigate any unintended consequences? Could I really develop objective, quantified data to reach final judgments on the client's behavioral changes? Could I apply my metrics background to support an assessment of post-coaching behavioral changes? How else could I get what I needed to move forward? These questions helped me identify two additional options.

Option 3: I wanted to increase my internal professional comfort level with confidentiality if I was going to work for this organization. I began to question whether the high standard of confidentiality I used in my practice was necessary in this situation. I realized that I could ask for an explanation of what the organization expected in the final written reports and check in with the client to be coached on the acceptability of this contract element. I could ask the organization to allow my clients to review what I proposed in my report. I was anticipating discussions with my clients like the dialogue that can take place in a performance review. That included questioning the accuracy of the information, adding new information, challenging generalizations of the information, exploring the usefulness of the information, and considering how a third party could possibly interpret the information.

Option 4: And as noted above, I do not believe the coach is the best qualified to judge the success of the coaching engagement. There is some humility here, as I may not have observed, interpreted, or contextualized everything correctly. I believe the best source of information on any behavioral change comes from the people who work day in and day out with the client. While discussing this with my colleague, an option became obvious: I could ask for permission to implement a mini–stakeholder interview/survey at the conclusion of the engagement and use that as the basis for the final written report.

Act

After creating the above four options, I knew I had a solid framework for determining my next course of action.

- I asked for an example of a final written report and reviewed that with the director of the HROD office to make sure I understood what was liked in the example and what people reading the reports would be paying particular attention to.
- I rewrote that report into a template format and reviewed it with the client I was starting with. I received, without reservation, approval to use this in our coaching work.
- I asked and gained permission from the director of HROD to share the draft written report with my client in advance of submission. This worked for the organization

because I was attesting to the integrity and accuracy of the report.

- I proposed a mini–stakeholder interview/survey, anchored by the client's goals, to be conducted before final payment. This approach was fully embraced and has become the norm for this program. The final report template is included in Appendix F.
- I reviewed this case with my coaching colleague, and we discussed the changes to my contracting and how I needed to expand my concept of the value of coaching to more deeply embrace the impact on the organization.
- I went back to the challenge that I had previously set aside regarding money. The above resolution made that a moot point.

As this case example demonstrates, applying the RFDA model led me to be a better coach. I gave myself the space and time to deeply reflect on my decision process. And I was confident that I covered my personal and professional obligations as a coach. In this case, those obligations felt stronger when I considered how my written final reports—in addition to my coaching—had the potential to affect the long-term career of this client, as well other clients in this organization. I found it empowering to acknowledge the limits to what I could do as a coach. For example, I did not have the same observational data my client's coworkers had on the behavioral changes. It felt good to find a well-grounded solution to an ethical dilemma, one that led me to change how I evaluate a coaching engagement. This reflective process of working with a trusted colleague also gave me the opportunity to further explicate my own personal code of ethics as a coach. The potency of having the support of a colleague for this work of reflection-in-relationship led me to seek out the coaching supervisor training and certification program. During training in that program, I became aware that one of the highest-ranked professional dilemmas is "conflicting interests/agendas between the sponsoring organization and the client."[15]

Coach-Client-Manager Confidentiality Example

The manager of my client saw me in the building and approached me after I had finished a session with his subordinate. He asked, "What are you and [client] working on?"

Recognize

While this seemed to be a straightforward question, I wanted to pause, since my model of coaching includes several meetings with the client's manager—an introductory meeting on contracting and outcomes and a later meeting to assure alignment on the specific goals for the engagement. Since we had already completed both meetings, his question caused a blip on my radar. The effectiveness of all coaching is anchored by the relationship between the client and the coach in an environment where clients can fully access their critical thinking without being thwarted by defensiveness and are assured that the discussions will be held in strict confidence. I was unsure of the motivation for the manager's question. Why was he asking me this, rather than asking his subordinate? The facts were straightforward, but my somatic experience—the tension in my jaws—was still not relaxed. Was he hoping I would reveal something that his client was not sharing? Did something change in their relationship, their communication? Was the manager signaling a change in focus? Or was this just an innocent question expressing interest? I felt I was missing something and knew I did not understand what was behind his request. Using the RFDA model, I had to start by suspending any judgments and obtain information to make the best choices on how to proceed.

The benefit of using the RFDA model is that it provides a structured process for critical thinking. Maybe the manager's question did not pose an ethical dilemma. Maybe it was just a cleverly disguised opportunity to help the client and manager build a better relationship.

Frame

Rules: The guiding rules from various coaching associations are quite clear that coaches are obligated to the strictest levels of confidentiality and are expected to have clarified that in the contracting phase.[16] But providing a quick reminder of our confidentiality agreement and just replying, "That is an important question. Why don't you ask the client yourself?" did not feel like the right response to the manager's question.

Most good: Maybe a quick answer would miss an opportunity to build their relationship. Anchored by my curiosity, I started a short conversation with the manager on what he really wanted to know. I asked if he was asking out of interest or if something else was going on. He shared that his question was one driven by curiosity and by a desire to help. From what I knew of this manager, his explanation rang true. At our introductory meeting, he had shared his desire to help, and the client wholeheartedly agreed that that was his motivation. Even without knowing what "help" would look like, I knew keeping the manager involved could lead to better outcomes. It was easy to envision benefits in exploring how the client and the manager were thinking about the manager's involvement. Pursuing that would be morally consistent with how I saw myself as a coach.

Diagnose

The straightforward option 1 would be to encourage the manager to share that same desire to help with my client. Option 2 would be for me to broach this issue with my client. And option 3 would be for me to accept some responsibility for ensuring that the manager stayed involved throughout the coaching process.

I shifted from thinking about his question in such a literal way. Could I embellish my option 3 to involve the manager and the client and still ensure the confidentiality of the coaching engagement? What information would be appropriate for a mid-engagement progress check-in with the three of us? Could I enlist my client in developing the agenda for such a three-way meeting? I found that I had to refine my thinking about confidentiality. Over the years, I have identified two conditions under which I advise my clients to be cautious about what they share with bosses from our coaching conversations. The first is when they feel pressured to share. The second is when sharing could bring negative consequences.

Act

With the first three stages completed, I decided on a course of action.

- I talked with my client about how best to take advantage of the boss's offer of support, as well as his desire for an update.

- We set a three-way meeting to discuss the coaching engagement. During that meeting, I reaffirmed how I viewed the confidentiality of what was done in coaching. The manager shared his sincere desire to help and that he fully understood the importance of confidentiality. We discussed pressure to share and possible negative consequences of sharing.

The manager's comments, recognizing both sides of the issue, resulted in higher levels of trust and better boundary management between him and his direct report, whom he was grooming for a higher-level position. The meeting culminated in an articulation of process questions (frequency of meetings, level of engagement, etc.), content discussions (areas of success and of continued effort), and actionable ideas for support. My client thanked the boss for his support and expressed sincere appreciation for his engagement.

COMMON DILEMMAS

Some of the major ethical challenges I and other coaches have experienced fall into three categories: confidentiality, dual relationships, and coaching versus consulting.

Confidentiality

The ICF guideline on confidentiality includes two parts. First, the coach will ensure the protection of any information obtained during the coaching engagement unless consent to release is given. Second, the coach will make every effort to honor the client's confidentiality and, if in doubt, will consult an ICF certified mentor coach.

The case examples earlier in the chapter address the confidentiality challenges between the coach and the organization, as well as between the coach, client, and manager. Less obvious, but equally important, are how coaches handle information about the organization.

Proprietary Information

Most coaching engagements require some form of confidentiality agreement or nondisclosure agreement (NDA) in the contracting phase, which specifies that information learned about the organization through the coaching engagement will not be shared outside the coaching work. When your coaching engagements involve individuals at the executive level, this becomes significantly more important. When something is said that I believe could be proprietary, my simple question has always been, "Is what I just heard in the public domain?" While there have been times I got curious about proprietary information being disclosed, coaches are not paid to focus on the business. Rather, we get curious about how the business is affecting our client and how our client is influencing the business. I find the safest course of action is to err on the side of caution and treat the information as proprietary until I hear otherwise, which falls in the category of doing the most good.

Competing Organizations

As you coach at higher levels of an organization, it is important to be mindful of the organization's sensitivity to a coach working with a competing organization. For example, at one very large oil and gas company, they were direct: if you coach our executives, you cannot be coaching executives at companies A and B. While most organizations are not that direct, this example underscores the importance of respecting boundaries and of the coach's potential lack of knowledge/awareness of what the organization might consider proprietary. Working in several organizations in the same industry requires an extra level of awareness and sensitivity to the competitive landscape. While I felt okay coaching in different organizations across an industry, I also needed to abide by organizational rules and expectations.

Coach and Outside Others

In addition to proprietary information, the coach often is exposed to information that is not yet public knowledge or that the company just prefers not to be shared. While it can give the coach an ego boost to share such information in other contexts, doing so is not advised. Sharing information without the name of the organization may be okay; sharing information that includes the company's name crosses a line. A recent example centered around a luncheon conversation with friends on how various firms were exploring their options for COVID-19 vaccination requirements. To say, "This is how [a particular company] is looking at implementing a vaccination regimen" violates my core value of confidentiality and respect for the sensitive nature of the information. It could also be incorrect. Information we hear in client conversations is typically not shared because of how it could be construed or misconstrued in other contexts and because it may not be complete or even still current. By being cognizant of these issues, I am being respectful of ethical rules, my virtues, and my clients' rights.

Dual Relationships

A dual relationship may exist whenever there are multiple and possibly competing roles/interests between two or more individuals. This kind of relationship can most easily happen when the coach has more than one client at a given organization. The ICF guidelines on these potential conflicts of interest are to discuss them and resolve them with both the clients' and the sponsoring organization's best interest in mind.

While there are tremendous benefits to the coach of having multiple clients at one organization (e.g., understanding the cultural do's/don'ts, knowing the context, having the ability to connect the dots during the conversation by knowing the other players, etc.), the drawback is that those benefits come with the risks inherent in dual relationships. When the clients are in different departments and are at different levels, normal prudence and self-reminders of confidentiality suffice. Some of the areas that can create challenges are (1) clients who are in the same department, (2) one client who reports to another client, (3) the coach's relationship with the sponsor, and (4) being recruited to take on the system. I explore each of these four areas in the next sections. The dual relationship with both coaching and supervising internal clients has unique challenges. As I do not have first-hand experience in this area, I refer you to the excellent chapter "Supervising Internal Clients," in *Coaching and Mentoring Supervision.*[17]

Clients in the Same Department

When the clients are peers and they are receiving coaching, they may be potential competitors for the same higher-level positions. A collaborative relationship stimulates openness and trust; a competitive relationship can engender the opposite. The clients may also have the same boss.

I explore why the sponsor wants both executives to receive coaching at the same time and whether that has been explained to the two clients. If there is a hidden agenda, one involving some form of comparison or competition, that agenda could easily undermine the trust required for effective coaching. Even the appearance or the perception of a hidden agenda could have negative consequences for the relationship, the feedback environment, and the effectiveness of the coaching. Making sure there is no hidden agenda is being mindful of the common good and the coach's virtues.

Boss-Subordinate Relationship

Among my coaching colleagues, there is a blanket response to the dynamic of coaching both the boss and the boss's subordinate at the same time: don't do it. My experience confirms that advice. I was invited to coach both a manager and her direct report at the same time. With my sixth sense tingling and some desire to stay on positive terms, rather than giving a quick "no" response, I set up a three-way meeting to discuss the issue. I pushed back that coaches never know how the conversations will unfold or what issues will be surfaced. No matter how collegial they considered their relationship, I did not want the risk of getting triangulated or breaching confidentially. Coaches get triangulated when they inadvertently become a substitute for direct communication between a client and manager. We agreed to wait to start the second client until after the first engagement was complete. The source of ethical conflict was clear: How do you concurrently serve the best interests of both clients when those interests may be divergent? Working those dual interests in an environment marked by power imbalances presents significant boundary-management challenges. Avoiding such situations keeps the coach respectful of justice, rights, and virtue.

Coach and Sponsor

Another potential downside to having multiple clients in the same organization centers on the relationship between the coach and the organization sponsor or engagement manager. While the experience can be beneficial for all parties, there are risks of perceived favoritism by individual clients and of lower standards for coaches. The risk of favoritism in the assignment of coaches appears when the client does not have choice in selecting their coach. When the organization assigns the coach, it is typically drawing from a pool of prequalified coaches.

The potential effect on the quality of coaching comes from the organization's standards. My experience has been that once coaches are admitted to a coaching pool, the organization does not critically evaluate their performance, require them to take continuing professional development courses (CPDs), or require them to be in a supervisory relationship. Over time, any of these could result in a lowering of the quality of coaching. Coaches may not want the organization to critically evaluate their performance or require CPDs or supervision, but that is exactly what should be happening. The lack of attentiveness could have unfavorable consequences for the organization. While coaches work to benefit the client, we also work for the organization and are best served by attending to the needs of all parties (i.e., considering our virtues and what does the most good).

Coaching with a System View

Coaches can find themselves exposed to values and behaviors that are not consonant with their internal values, and these can be particularly visible when working with multiple clients at a single organization. As Simon Western notes, "Coaching can bring ethical dilemmas to life, noticing how gender, race, sexuality and disability issues are played out in the workplace."[18] In one engagement, my client complained that his request for an internal hire was being held up by HR as he was trying to bypass the internal requirements of interviewing two outside candidates, one of which should be a minority. He was upset by this "injustice" because he had a great record on diversity issues. Because I coached others in this organization, I was fairly attuned to why the organization put this diversity guidance in place. I was able to see the organization from a broader perspective and invited a deeper conversation, including why the organization might have put these requirements in place. That conversation also covered his position as a role model for the more junior executives. The conversation helped my client see why the organization was doing what it did and the consequences his actions had outside his department.

The coach is in a position, as someone outside the system, to see ethical dilemmas objectively. If you find yourself working in an environment in which discrimination is okay, how do you define your role? You may be in a position to influence. One way of influencing is to shine a light on the moral question with the client and/or the sponsor. If the issue isn't of concern to either the client or the organization, things get stickier. Are the issues of a magnitude that will prevent you from being fully engaged and present with your client? Are there actions being taken that are addressing the situation that you might not be aware of? Are you conformable continuing to work in this organization? Being mindful of justice and virtue is helpful in these cases.

Coaching, Consulting, and Cocreating

The ICF defines *coaching* as "partnering with clients in a thought-provoking and creative process that inspires them to maximize their personal and professional potential."[19] Consulting, in my opinion and that of many of my colleagues, is serving as a subject-matter expert to solve the client's problems. I think of the coaching role as one in which trust is built on a relationship of care for the development of the client and the consulting role as one in which the trust is built by applying expert subject-matter knowledge. Under the ICF criteria for advanced certification, for a coach to offer solutions is not acceptable, except in rare cases. Doing so could disqualify the applicant from advanced certification.[20]

Cocreating Solutions

Both research on how adults learn[21] and experience conclude that we learn best when we are intrinsically motivated to learn, are active participants in the learning process, have opportunities to apply what we have learned, and are encouraged to reflect on what we have learned. In my view, coaches are serving as equal partners when they are actively involved in cocreating possible solutions and providing the space for reflection. Adding cocreating pushes the ICF definition. It is also shy of the consulting definition because it moves from providing answers to providing the context to generate the best set of possible solutions. In practice, cocreation requires a higher level of self-awareness and personal integrity on the part of the coach. I think in terms of both parties putting the best information on the table and then sifting through and blending those ideas to develop the best solution (i.e., do the most good).

Power Differential

Being in a cocreating relationship requires working collaboratively as colleagues, not in an unequal power relationship. The rub in this blurred coach/consultant approach is the potential power differential between the client and the coach. I work hard to avoid this power imbalance from the very beginning, in the contracting phase. I knew I was not successful once when a client jokingly said, "So, I know I'm really screwed up. Think you can fix me?" Even when said in a joking way, this raises a red flag. That is why offering possible solutions requires good up-front contracting, soft hands, and a large dose of cautiousness. Frequently, clients find it too easy to sit back and let the coach do the heavy lifting. The coach enables that dynamic by sliding into the consultancy mode. This is a perfect opportunity for the coach to make that observation directly: "You seem quite comfortable with me coming up with a lot of the ideas. How do you see this?" The coach must be ever vigilant to ensure parity of engagement and avoid creating a dependency relationship with the client. Doing this honors justice, virtue, and rights.

Deeper Understanding

Being in a cocreating relationship also requires a willingness on the part of the client to explore deeper understanding of the issues. For example, before offering possible solutions, the coach should be attuned to why a client is not coming up with their own ideas. In a recent interchange, after suggesting an option involving the client directly asking her boss something, I asked her for an example of another possible solution. After we had a robust pool of options and before acting on those, I followed up by asking what made coming up with solutions hard for her. The thinking behind the question was to deepen her insight into her own assumptions, to hold them up for reflection. The challenge is not whether I add to the pool of possible solutions; rather, it is whether I use a process that helps the client grow. This kind of conversation, because it can be so uncomfortable, requires a deep investment in the client as an adult learner who has the internal resources to solve challenging issues. It honors the coach's virtues and the clients' rights.

Self-Awareness

Being in a cocreating relationship requires coaches to examine their own motives. I want to make sure my motives are solidly in cocreation and not coming from impatience or ego satisfaction. Sometimes a client needs a nudge to prime the pump and get their thoughts flowing. After giving that nudge is a good time to back away and give them the creative space they need. Sometimes, I find myself impatient with the pace of change. At other times, I may feel the pull to show off what I know. Coaches' motives matter, as does an awareness of straying from a cocreating mode into one of creating a dependency relationship that undermines learning (which would go against a coach's virtues).

The goal of this chapter is to explore the ethical dilemmas inherent in coaching and to provide a process for addressing those dilemmas that adds clarity and depth to a personal code of ethics. The RFDA model was developed to help graduate students with ethics. In this chapter, RFDA is adapted to the ethical dilemmas faced by coaches to increase their pool of explicit ethical knowledge and create an expanded personal code of ethical behavior.

Appendix A: Seven-Stage Roadmap

SEVEN-STAGE MODEL	
STAGE	**DESCRIPTION AND DELIVERABLE**
1. Establish Relationship	Meet the executive, review the coaching process, and determine the mutual benefit of entering into a coaching contract. Clarify what it means to work in a safe, bounded, goal-directed relationship.
2. Frame Change Intent	Guide the executive in creating an explicit statement of three or four goals that have the full support of the executive's sponsor.
3. Engage Feedback Support Team	Conduct the Stakeholder Feedback Interviews. Review the goal-directed feedback report with the executive.
4. Commit to Action	Complete the Commit to Action Worksheet that includes (1) the key areas for behavioral development, (2) specific actions to create change, (3) an action learning project, and (4) an action plan.
5. Measure Success	At approximately five months into a six-month coaching engagement, the client asks the same feedback support team to reevaluate the driving and restraining forces to his goals.
6. Sustain Progress	Meet with the executive and the executive's sponsor to provide a high-level overview of progress and to build in ongoing support from the sponsor.
7. Provide Feedback to Coach	The executive evaluates the coach against goals that were important to the coach.

TIME LINE FOR A TYPICAL SIX-MONTH ENGAGEMENT

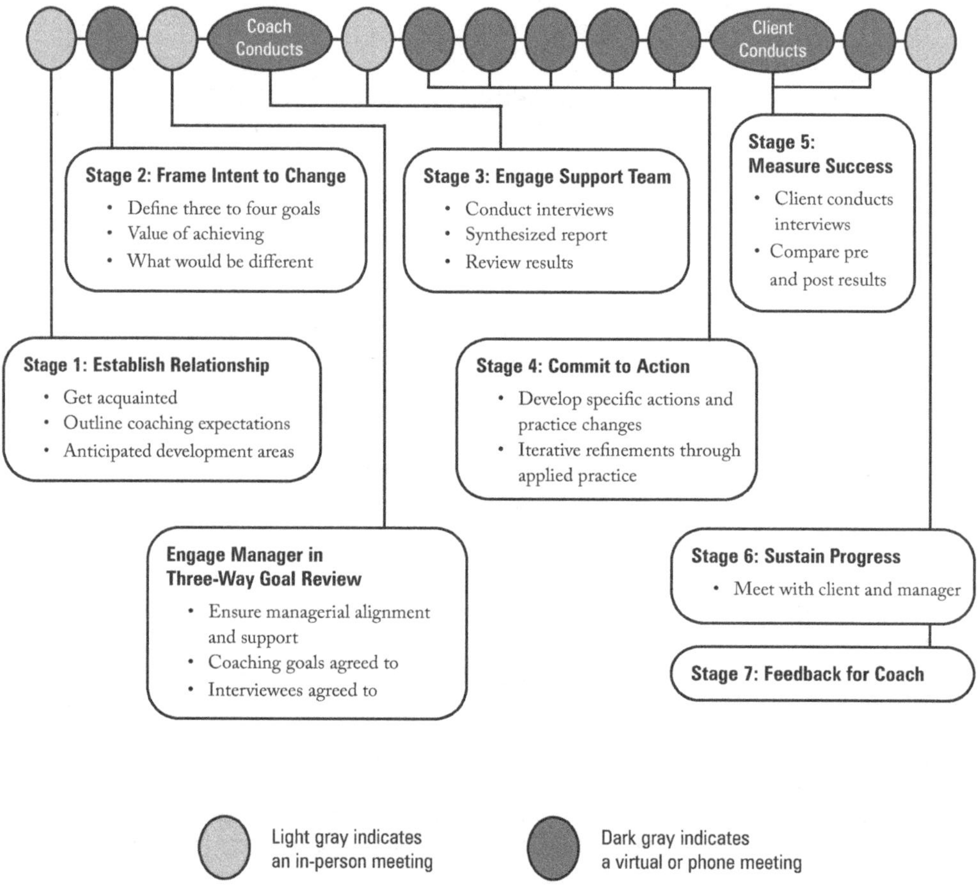

Coach Conducts

Client Conducts

Stage 1: Establish Relationship

- Get acquainted
- Outline coaching expectations
- Anticipated development areas

Stage 2: Frame Intent to Change

- Define three to four goals
- Value of achieving
- What would be different

Engage Manager in Three-Way Goal Review

- Ensure managerial alignment and support
- Coaching goals agreed to
- Interviewees agreed to

Stage 3: Engage Support Team

- Conduct interviews
- Synthesized report
- Review results

Stage 4: Commit to Action

- Develop specific actions and practice changes
- Iterative refinements through applied practice

Stage 5: Measure Success

- Client conducts interviews
- Compare pre and post results

Stage 6: Sustain Progress

- Meet with client and manager

Stage 7: Feedback for Coach

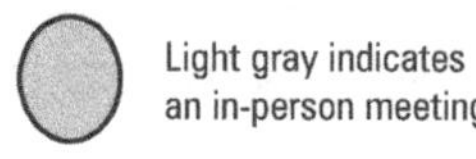
Light gray indicates an in-person meeting

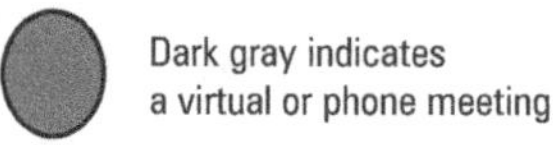
Dark gray indicates a virtual or phone meeting

STAGE 1: ESTABLISH RELATIONSHIP WORKSHEET

Contract Expectations

-
-
-

Agreements to Build Safety

-
-
-

Duration of Engagement

Meeting Frequency

Client Contact Information

Sponsor Contact Information

Administrative Contact Information

Notes

STAGE 2: CHANGE INTENT WORKSHEET

Pressing Business Issues

-
-
-

Personal Leadership Challenges

-
-
-

Executive Career Aspirations

-
-
-

Areas of Known Strengths

-
-
-

Potential Goals

-
-
-

STAGE 2: CHANGE INTENT WORKSHEET, CONTINUED

GOAL	VALUE OF ACHIEVING	WHAT WOULD BE DIFFERENT

STAGE 3: ENGAGE FEEDBACK SUPPORT TEAM WORKSHEET

GOAL	
Driving forces →	← Restraining forces
GOAL	
Driving forces →	← Restraining forces
GOAL	
Driving forces →	← Restraining forces
GOAL	
Driving forces →	← Restraining forces

STAGE 4: COMMIT TO ACTION PREWORK AND REFLECTION WORKSHEET

BEHAVIOR OF FOCUS			
Impact of My Behavior	**Why I'm Tempted *Not* to Change**	**How to Catch Myself**	**What I Will Do Differently**
Brand or reputation: Morale of team or self: Efficiency or productivity: Long-term risk exposure: Delivering the best product: Bottom-line impact:	These behaviors were developed for good reasons. What were those? What benefits do you get from continuance? What potential downsides are you trying to avoid? What makes this hard to not do?	What am I doing? What am I thinking? What is going on inside me? Who else sees this? How can I recruit them to help me?	What am I willing to commit to do? Where am I willing to do this? Who am I willing to share this with? When will I bring this into our coaching work?

STAGE 4: COMMIT TO ACTION WORKSHEET

GOAL

Key Areas for Development	Specific Actions (sufficient?)	Action Learning Project (where practice?)

GOAL

Key Areas for Development	Specific Actions (sufficient?)	Action Learning Project (where practice?)

GOAL

Key Areas for Development	Specific Actions (sufficient?)	Action Learning Project (where practice?)

GOAL

Key Areas for Development	Specific Actions (sufficient?)	Action Learning Project (where practice?)

STAGE 5: MEASURE SUCCESS WORKSHEET

GOAL		MAJOR DIFFERENCES TO ORIGINAL FORCE FIELD
Driving forces →	← Restraining forces	
GOAL		
Driving forces →	← Restraining forces	
GOAL		
Driving forces →	← Restraining forces	
GOAL		
Driving forces →	← Restraining forces	

STAGE 6: SUSTAIN PROGRESS WORKSHEET

GOAL	WHAT IS DIFFERENT?	HOW CAN YOUR MANAGER SUPPORT YOUR PROGRESS?

Appendix B:
Shareholder Feedback Interview Protocol

Feedback Support Team Participant:
Date:
Phone:

Thank you for making your time available. I am an executive coach working with [executive's first/last name]. [First name] has an overarching goal of increasing his leadership effectiveness in order to [insert the high level goal—e.g., create a sustainable business, one that delivers results today and builds for tomorrow]. He values your input.

I would like to explain the process I use, as this will help you respond. It will also give you some insight into this process in case you want to use it yourself. I use a very specific approach to gathering usable feedback, one that increases the validity and usability of the information gathered. I do this in three ways.

- First, I focus the conversation on [first name's] goals. This assures that your feedback is on target with what is most important to [first name].

- Second, I will ask for behaviors you have observed and the impact of those behaviors on you and the business. This grounds the feedback on data and gives insight into specific things that he or she can change.

- Third, I look for those behaviors that are driving forces to achieving the goal, and then I look for those behaviors that are restraining forces to achieving the goal. This provides a "systems view" and enables [first name] and I to quickly prioritize the most important behaviors to target for enhancing or changing.

In addition to the goals detailed by [first name], there are three broad topics I build into this interview:

1. Identify any profound strengths.

2. Identify any fatal flaws or career derailers.

3. What else?

Your comments and those of others I am interviewing will be reviewed with [first name] during our executive coaching sessions. At the end of this interview, I will ask your permission to share your verbatim comments with [first name]. I ask at the end, as then you will know what you have said! [humor]

Any questions before we begin?

GOAL 1

Driving forces: behaviors that help

NOTE: Read the goal and ask, "What are the behaviors or activities you see from [executive's first name] that move him/her toward achieving this goal?

Q: What did you see her doing that led you to say that?

Q: And the business impact of that?

Restraining forces: behaviors that hinder

NOTE: Refresh on the goal and ask, "What are the behaviors or activities you see from [executive's first name] that move him/her away from achieving this goal?

Q: What would be another example?

Q: How does this behavior impact the team or business?

Q: Do I have this right, when she does . . . , then . . . happens?

GOAL 2

Driving forces: behaviors that help

NOTE: Read the goal and ask, "What are the behaviors or activities you see from [executive's first name] that move him/her toward achieving this goal?

Q: What was the impact of that?

Q: What is an example?

Restraining forces: behaviors that hinder

NOTE: Refresh on the goal and ask, "What are the behaviors or activities you see from [executive's first name] that move him/her away from achieving this goal?

Q: Do you know if she is aware of this behavior?

Q: Can you point to an example?

GOAL 3

Driving forces: behaviors that help

NOTE: Read the goal and ask, "What are the behaviors or activities you see from [executive's first name] that move him/her toward achieving this goal?

Q: It is an important message as his or her boss that you are seeing so few driving examples. Is she aware you see her that way?

Q: What do you see when you say he or she is good at . . . ?

Restraining forces: behaviors that hinder

NOTE: Refresh on the goal and ask, "What are the behaviors or activities you see from [executive's first name] that move him/her away from achieving this goal?

Q: Where do you see this?

Q: Is there an example that would really nail this for [first name]?

GOAL 4

Driving forces: behaviors that help

NOTE: Read the goal and ask, "What are the behaviors or activities you see from [executive's first name] that move him/her toward achieving this goal?

Q: Is there an example he or she would recognize?

Q: How does this drive him or her towards the goal?

Restraining forces: behaviors that hinder

NOTE: Refresh on the goal and ask, "What are the behaviors or activities you see from [executive's first name] that move him/her away from achieving this goal?

Q: Is there a recent example of where you have seen this?

Q: Anything else?

PROFOUND STRENGTHS:

Are there things [first name] does that might be considered a profound strength—something in the top tenth percentile?

DERAILERS:

Are there things [first name] does that could lead to career derailment or less than full success in current or future roles?

Q: Are there examples where you could identify the negative impact of acting this way?

Q: Is this a new behavior or one that has been around awhile?

OPEN-ENDED QUESTION (TIME PERMITTING):

What else would be important for [first name] to hear?

Thank you for your time and insights. These will be helpful to [first name] as he/she works on enhancing his/her leadership effectiveness.

Do I have your permission to share my notes on our conversation with him/her?

Appendix C: Stakeholder Feedback Interview Summary Report

PREPARED FOR

NAME OF EXECUTIVE

BY

NAME OF COACH

DATE

PROCESS REVIEW

This report reflects the information gained through interviews with [number] interviewees, encompassing direct reports, peers, managers, and executive-level leaders. Those were: ______________________

____.

These individuals were selected based on their contemporary knowledge of the client, their having the client's best interest at heart, and their willingness to speak candidly. Prior to starting the interviews, the list of people interviewed was reviewed and approved by the client's manager, ______________________.

The methodology for the interviews is an integral part of a goal-focused coaching model. Details of the theory and process used in the interviews are documented in the book *Transformational Executive Coaching: A Relationship-Based Model for Sustained Change*, by Ted Middelberg.

This report follows the format of identifying both the driving and the restraining forces for each of the coaching goals. Themes from the interviews are identified, each theme followed by several example quotes. The goals were developed with the client based on available information, with consideration of pressing leadership issues, career interests, and the leadership needs of the organization. The goals were reviewed and approved by the client's manager. The report also includes responses to three open-ended questions. The responses to the open-ended questions are included in their entirety.

Everyone interviewed agreed to have the interviewer share with [name of client] the notes taken during those interviews. They also agreed to serve as a resource for ongoing feedback to [name of client].

For each participant in the stakeholder interviews, a complete transcript of the notes taken during the conversation is appended as a separate section of this report.

GOAL 1

Driving forces: behaviors that help	**Restraining forces: behaviors that hinder**
Theme 1:	Theme 1:
•	•
•	•
•	•
Theme 2	Theme 2:
•	•
•	•
•	•
Theme 3:	Theme 3:
•	•
•	•
•	•

Repeat the above format of driving and restraining forces for each of the remaining goals.

PROFOUND STRENGTHS

Are there things [client name] does that might be considered a profound strength? How would you finish the sentence: "Wow, this person is really, really good at . . ."?

Participant	Comments

DERAILERS

Are there things [client name] does that might prevent them from being fully successful in their current role? Or affect their future success at [name of organization]? Or even lead to derailment?

Participant	Comments

OPEN-ENDED QUESTION (TIME PERMITTING)	
What else would be important for [client] to hear?	
Participant	**Comments**

Appendix D: Evidence-Based Coaching Evaluation

I. COACHING SKILLS THAT ENABLE SUCCESS

1 = Strongly Disagree 3 = Neutral 5 = Strongly Agree

1. Has your coach established an environment marked by trust and open communication?

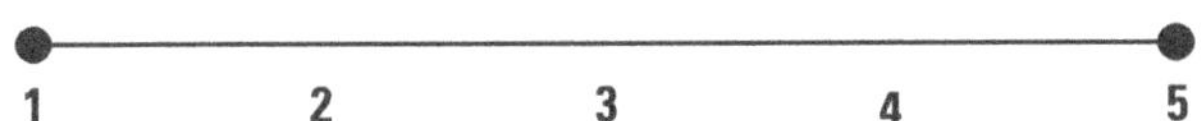

2. Does your coach show a genuine interest in your progress and success?

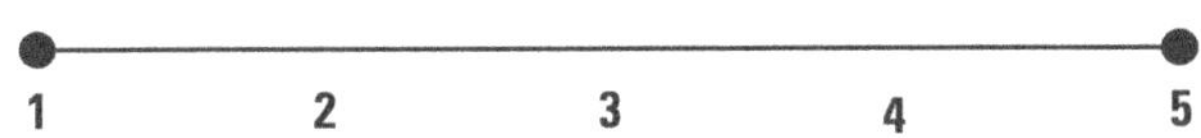

3. Does your coach provide relevant inputs and connect to your issues?

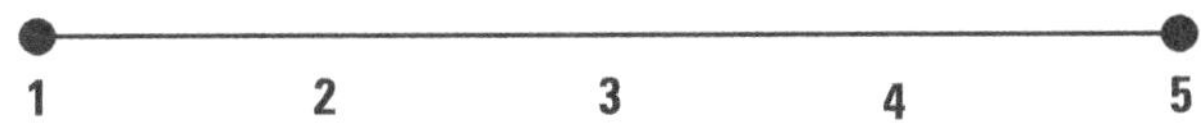

4. Does your coach hold you accountable for your commitments?

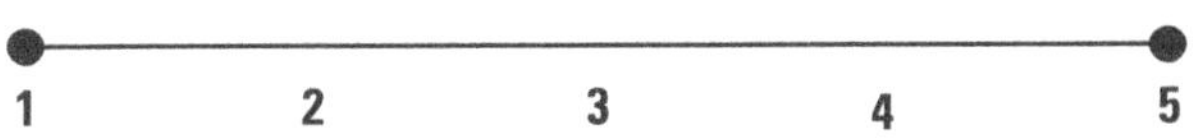

5. Does your coach stretch your comfort zone by asking important and challenging questions?

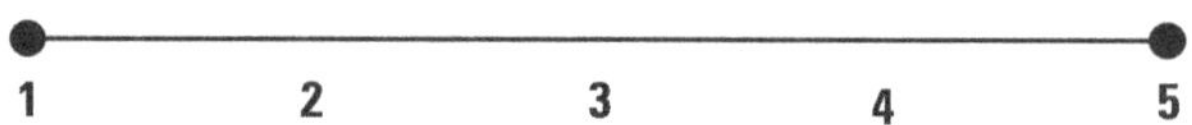

6. How would you rate your overall satisfaction with your coaching experience?

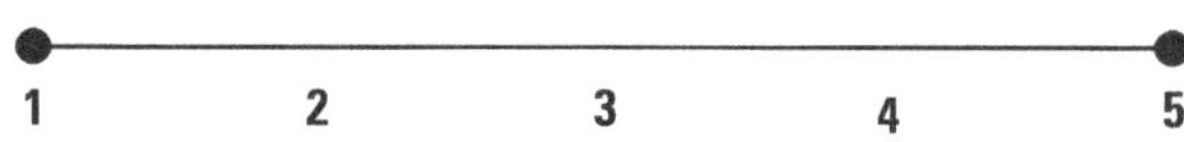

II. COACHING EXPERIENCE

Coaching is intended to provide a safe environment and trusting relationship to foster improved performance in a sustainable way.

1. What did your coach do that worked well and should be continued?

2. What did your coach do that did not work well or could be improved?

III. COACHING CRITICAL INCIDENT OR "AH-HA" MOMENT

Describe a critical incident or "ah-ha" moment you had during the coaching engagement. This could be a moment of special insight or new ways of seeing yourself/others. This could also be a pivot point, when you made commitments to new behaviors or actions.

IV. OUTCOME METRICS

1 = Strongly Disagree 3 = Neutral 5 = Strongly Agree

1. The coaching helped me improve as a leader.

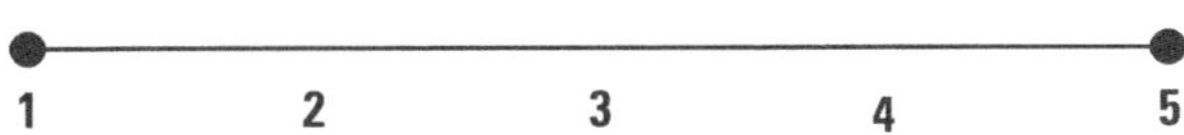

2. The coaching experience was worth my time.

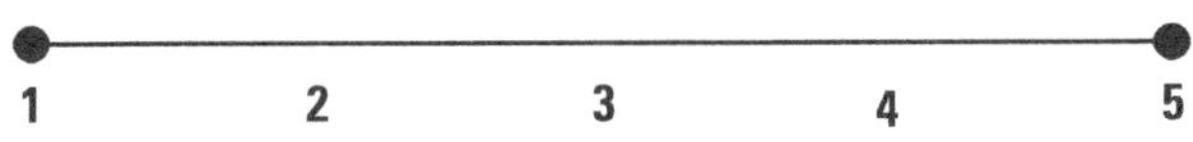

3. As a result of coaching, I have improved one or more critical business metrics.

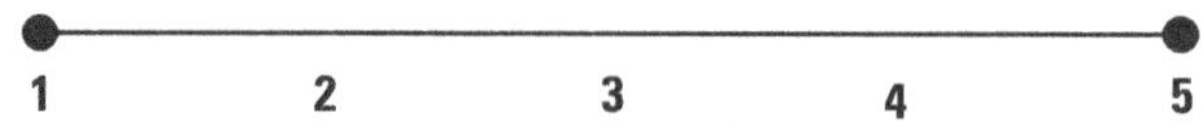

4. Coaching is intended to provide value to both you and the organization. How would you describe that value?

End of Evaluation

Appendix E: Mini–Stakeholder Interview and Final Coaching Report

MINI–STAKEHOLDER INTERVIEW

Advance Email to Set Up a Meeting

Hi, [Name] [*Sending separate memos is more personal, and the participants do not see who else you selected.*]

I am committed to improving my leadership capabilities and would like your support.

I am working with my executive coach to help me enhance my leadership effectiveness. As part of that process, I would like to gain your inputs on specific areas that I have targeted. The interview will be conducted [at my office or via phone] and will take thirty minutes.

No preparation is required. I will share my goals and ask you to identify behaviors that are helping me achieve my targeted goals and behaviors that may be getting in the way of achieving my targeted goals. I am especially interested in areas where you have seen progress and areas that still need attention.

In advance, thank you.

Opening Comments to Begin the Interview

Again, thank you for meeting with me and offering your support to help me further refine my leadership effectiveness skills. As I shared earlier, this conversation is about the leadership goals I have been working on.

First, for each of my goals, I will ask you to identify behaviors that are helping me achieve that goal and to identify behaviors that may still be getting in the way of achieving that goal.

Second, I will ask you to rate my progress over the past six months and provide tips on how to make further improvements.

Third, I will ask if you see any leading-edge leadership issues that could be important for my continued success.

Any questions before we begin?

Note: A best practice is to preprint and use the attached forms to capture notes. You will not have time to ask all the prompting questions, but use them when they make sense.

GOAL 1

Driving forces: behaviors that help	**Restraining forces: behaviors that hinder**
My first goal is [state goal]. What have you seen me doing that moves me closer to achieving this goal?	And on the other side, what gets in the way? What are the behaviors you see from me that move me away from achieving this goal?
Q: Is there an example you could point to?	Q: What would be another example?
Q: What did you see me doing that led you to say that?	Q: How does this behavior impact the team or business?
Q: And the business impact of that?	

What overall rating would you give (1 = very low; 5 = very high)?
And what could I do to move your rating up a notch?

GOAL 2

Driving forces: behaviors that help

As before, on my second goal of [state goal], what examples would you point to where I am doing things that are helping me achieve this goal?

Q: What was the impact of that?

Q: What is an example?

Restraining forces: behaviors that hinder

And on the other side, what gets in the way? What are the things you see me doing that are getting in the way of my achieving this goal?

Q: That was helpful. Are there other examples you would point to?

What overall rating would you give (1 = very low; 5 = very high)?
And what could I do to move your rating up a notch?

GOAL 3

Driving forces: behaviors that help

My third goal is [state goal]. What have you observed me doing that helps move me toward achieving this goal?

Q: Anything else?

Q: When you say I am good at that, what are you paying attention to? What is an example?

Restraining forces: behaviors that hinder

Still talking about my third goal of [state goal], what am I doing that is getting in the way of achieving this goal?

Q: Where do you see this?

Q: What else do you see me doing that gets in the way?

What overall rating would you give (1 = very low; 5 = very high)?
And what could I do to move your rating up a notch?

GOAL 4

Driving forces: behaviors that help

The goal is [state goal]. What examples would you point to where we are doing things that help move us toward achieving this goal?

Q: What was the impact of that?

Q: What is an example?

Restraining forces: behaviors that hinder

And on the other side, what gets in the way? What are the things you see me doing that are getting in the way of my achieving this goal?

Q: Can you point to an example?

Q: Are there other examples you would point to?

What overall rating would you give (1 = very low; 5 = very high)? And what could I do to move your rating up a notch?

LEADING-EDGE ISSUES

What are the leading-edge leadership issues that would be important for me to be aware of?

-
-
-

Thank you for your time and insights. These will be helpful to me as I work with my coach to further enhance my leadership effectiveness.

I would like your ongoing feedback when you see me doing things that either help or hinder, especially on the things that hinder or get in the way. Can I ask you to help by doing that?

Again, thank you!

FINAL COACHING REPORT

For: [name of executive]
Coach: [name of coach]

Process Overview

A small group of people were interviewed by [client's first name] to provide a snapshot on the leadership changes he has been working on over the past months. Those interviews had three parts.

- First, for each of his coaching goals, they were asked for examples of both the positive and the negative things they have observed.
- Second, they also were asked to rate his progress (1 = very low; 5 = very high) and to provide tips on how to make further improvements.
- Third, they were asked for any leading-edge leadership issues that would be important for [client's first name]'s continued success.

Outcome Overview

All those interviewed pointed to positive examples where they have seen improvements in his targeted behaviors. The additional attention [first name] has given to [first goal] is reflected in the following improvements. [Provide examples.] Similarly, the efforts [first name] has made over the past year on his goal of [second goal] are reflected in the positive outcomes of [provide outcomes examples]. Finally, on his goal of [third goal], the outcomes included [identify the outcomes/impact].

When asked for tips on how [first name] could further improve, participants made several suggestions, including [list key suggestions].

Coach's Observations

[First name] has been actively engaged in improving his leadership effectiveness through this coaching process. And the results are beginning to show. These gains have been made possible by [first name] making deliberate efforts and focusing his attention on these goals. My opinion is that there are three leading-edge issues that will benefit [first name] and the organization:

-
-
-

It has been my pleasure to have worked with [first and last name] over the past year.

[Coach's name and signature]

GOAL 1

Examples of things [client] has done that have helped (driving forces)	Examples of things [client] has done that got in the way (restraining forces)
•	•
•	•
•	•

And what could he do to move that rating up a notch?

GOAL 2

Examples of things [client] has done that have helped (driving forces)	Examples of things [client] has done that got in the way (restraining forces)
•	•
•	•
•	•

And what could he do to move that rating up a notch?

GOAL 3

Examples of things [client] has done that have helped (driving forces)	Examples of things [client] has done that got in the way (restraining forces)
•	•
•	•
•	•

And what could he do to move that rating up a notch?

LEADING-EDGE ISSUES

What are the leading-edge leadership issues that would be important for [first name] to be aware of?

-
-
-
-

End of Report

Appendix F: Three Group Supervision Models

Three very different models of group supervision are provided. They differ by qualifications for entry of the participants and training of the facilitator, by range of permissible topics, and by how the conversations are structured. They are similar in that these are self-forming around shared interests, intended to be long-running, and have virtually no cost or fees for entry. The learning objective is to enhance our skills and practice by working on our shortcomings.

GUIDELINES AND PROCESS FOR COACHES BUILT ON THE PRINCIPLES OF A MASTER MIND GROUP

This model is anchored by the Master Mind concept of Napoleon Hill, who coined the phrase in his classic 1937 book *Think and Grow Rich*.[1] He believed that a group of like-minded, achievement-oriented individuals could dramatically leverage each other's success. In a Master Mind group, a small group of people with a common link meet on a regular basis to confidentially work on one another's challenges in a safe space for being vulnerable and for working on shortcomings. This model reflects the collective efforts of a small group of Austin, Texas, coaching colleagues who spent many hours communicating, piloting, documenting, and implanting this framework.[2] Some of the critical factors that led to consistent outcomes included the one-to-four ratio of trained facilitators to coaches for a ninety-minute meeting, putting the group needs ahead of individual needs, and an emphasis on being a contributor rather than simply taking from the group.

The benefits you can glean from these Master Mind group sessions include:

- You are listened to in a safe and nonjudgmental environment.
- You have the support and encouragement of your fellow coaches.
- You dramatically increase your chances of resolving your coaching topic because a group of people will assist you in brainstorming and action steps.
- You can bounce ideas off the group before you implement an action, saving yourself time, energy, money, and aggravation.
- You receive helpful feedback from proactive, objective people who are invested in your success.
- You develop deeper relationships with other coaches.

Intentions

The intention is that this group will be used to provide a forum for brilliant thinking about a topic each coach brings to the Master Mind process. Any coaching-related topic is acceptable. Possible topics include:

- Management issues: keeping track of coaching hours, taking notes during the coaching session, preparing for coaching calls, etc.
- Professional development: evaluating your coaching effectiveness, maintaining a focus on your learning goals, etc.
- Interaction with clients: dealing with a client who does not take action or seems stuck, talks a lot, is consistently late for sessions, etc.
- Building your coaching business: developing business plan, deciding how to target potential client groups, developing a reference source, etc.
- Business marketing: website support, social media, branding, etc.

Operational Guidelines

1. Membership is open to active coaches who can commit to meet face-to-face on a regular basis (pre-COVID-19).
2. The goal of the group is to provide problem-solving opportunities and increase creativity among coaches and to provide a safe, constructive environment in which coaches can examine their coaching challenges, personal coaching goals, or any coaching-related issues for which they would like input.

3. Each group will be composed of four to six coaches. Each coach will have a total of twelve to fifteen minutes: two to three minutes to present their item, eight to nine minutes to receive feedback, and two to three minutes to share their takeaways.

4. Each group will be supported by at least one experienced facilitator.

Individual Coach's Responsibility

1. Each coach is responsible for completing the preparation form (shown later in this section) to maximize the interaction time in the group.

2. Each coach will be prepared to ask for the kind of input they want from the group—encouragement, support, critique, brainstorming possibilities/strategies, and so on.

3. After each coach has received feedback, they will state what they have received from the group. They may request additional information from specific group members to be shared later.

4. The presenting coach will take notes to record the strategies and suggestions generated by the brainstorming coaches.

Group's Responsibility

1. Group members will stay focused on one person's issue at a time.

2. Group members will listen to the speaker's issue/goal and ask questions to ensure clarity before offering feedback.

3. The facilitator will check to see that the whole group has a shared understanding of the issue/goal before offering feedback.

4. Group members will keep the feedback constructive.

5. The group will move quickly from one coach to another so that lots of ideas/possibilities can be generated without stepping on someone's thinking.

6. Group members will keep conversations confidential.

7. The group will enforce group norms.

Facilitator's Responsibility

An experienced facilitator is assigned to balance the open admission criteria. We employed a two-to-six or one-to-four ratio of facilitators to coaches for a ninety-minute meeting. The facilitators were coaches who had experience in the facilitation role and in managing group processes, placing the needs of the group above the needs of any one individual. Facilitators:

1. Keep the group focused on the presenter's request
2. Serve as timekeeper so that each associate has time to present and receive feedback
3. Monitor the sharing of the conversation space
4. Develop a means (e.g., Google Doc) for collecting experiences, testimonials, issues, etc.
5. Recruit and support new volunteer facilitators

Everyone's Responsibility

1. Everyone will monitor the group for issues, concerns, and opportunities for enhancements.
2. Everyone will ensure confidentiality of any individual's information.
3. Everyone will ensure a dynamically evolving process that meets the needs of the group.

Process

Round 1

The presenting coach shares the issue, problem, goal, question, idea, or proposal for consideration with the group from their preparation form. The coach can also share what has already been attempted to solve their presented topic. (Two to three minutes.)

Round 2

Group members ask clarifying questions. Helping the presenting coach get clear about his or her situation assures that the possibilities generated by the group are in alignment with the needs of the presenting coach. This is much like establishing the coaching agreement with a client. (One to two minutes.)

Round 3

The presenting coach asks for the kind of input wanted from the group—encouragement, support, critique, strategies, possibilities, shared experiences, and the like. (One minute.)

Round 4

This round is when the presenting coach will take notes on any comments, solutions, possibilities, and suggestions provided by the group. This is not a time for dialogue or storytelling. Group members share their best thinking, and the ideas flow from one member to another as they occur. The presenting coach simply listens while actively taking notes. The presenting coach controls this process and may signal to the group to stop the input process if he or she has gotten the desired outcome before the end of the allotted time. (Seven to eight minutes.)

Round 5

The presenting coach shares his or her takeaways and/or requests more time or information from specific group members based on input. (This conversation would take place later.) Group participants offer any additional assistance they are willing to provide the coach outside the meeting (processes, resources, contacts, time, etc.). (One to two minutes.)

The group then rotates to the next presenting coach and repeats the process.

Preparation and Reflection Form

Step 1

Write the topic you will be presenting for group consideration. Try to be concise, using only one to two sentences to get to the heart of your issue. It could be a concern, a challenge, an opportunity, an issue, a goal, a question, an idea, or a recurring problem that is becoming more troublesome. Remember: the problem named is the problem solved.

Topic: ____

____

____

Step 2

What is it you want from the group (alternative solutions, strategies, affirmations, support, examples, deep questioning, ideas)?

Request to group: ____

____

____

Step 3:

What are you taking away from the group's input?

____

____

____

Who in the group, if anyone, do you want to have additional conversation with?

____

____

____

Possible next steps: ______________________________

____

____

GUIDELINES AND PROCESS FOR GROUP SUPERVISION

This is a model of group supervision that was adapted for coaches by David Clutterbuck[3] and requires a skilled coaching supervisor as the facilitator. The following notes reflect actual sessions facilitated by Damian Goldvarg. Membership is restricted to members of the same coaching supervisor certification program. The key learning objective is for the participants to deepen their understanding of the models they are using to frame and reflect on the case.

Coaching Supervision Pre-session Preparation

Date:

Coach's Name:

How will I center and assure full availability for this work today?

- Select an eight- to ten-minute mindfulness meditation
- Quick check on how I am feeling about this session

How will I prepare for this meeting?

- Decide how I want to show up in this session
- Set one or two things to work on or get better at
- Review two or three models to possibly apply

Process

Logistics

Leader: Skilled coaching supervisor
Membership: Limited to participants in a coaching supervision certification program
Attending: Quick note of who was not able to attend and why

Opening

We bring our working energy into the room with a simple and functional check-in. The leader asks, "What are you doing that is interesting, and do you have a case you want to work on today?" The leader keeps track to ensure that no one is skipped. The leader reminds the members of the time boundaries and structure for today's meeting (e.g., two case studies and a discussion on marketing).

First Case Presentation

Setup

The leader gives us the template for our work. After the case presenter describes the case and what he or she wants, the members of the group are to provide comments and reflections and end with a question for the presenter to consider. The leader asks everyone to think about the models they are using to frame and reflect on the case. The presenter is guided to listen and, after everyone adds their inputs, to select the question or area of inquiry that will be most useful for him or her. The presenter asks if everyone is okay if he or she takes notes, rather than trying to sustain eye contact.

Discussion and Questions

Each person shares what is surfacing for them. The leader does so last. Questions fall into multiple "eyes," using Peter Hawkins's seven-eyed model (see details later in this section).[4]

Follow-Up to Group Input

The leader asks the presenter what they found particularly valuable and important for them to consider. After those comments, there is a check-in on whether the presenter got what they wanted and how they are now seeing this case.

Break

Didactic Lite

The leader asks everyone for the mental models they found useful as they were thinking about this and other cases. This is a great reminder to use and share the models to ensure we are thinking from multiple reference points. For example, models include:

- Hawkins's seven-eyed model (see below)
- Psychodynamic frames (borderline behaviors, splitting, attachment disorders, ego strength and development)
- Eric Berne's transactional analysis (parent, adult, and child ego states)
- Insight-generating techniques (white-boarding and metaphor exploration)
- Karpman drama triangle (persecutor, rescuer, victim)
- David Kolb's learning model (concrete, reflection, abstract, experiment)
- Kubler-Ross Change Curve (denial, anger, bargaining, depression, acceptance)

Second Case Presentation

This is an open and flowing conversation, rather than a fixed-order rotation that uses a "you get to speak only once" format. This is almost like a combination group brainstorm and facilitated discussion. Group members share their experiences, their techniques, and the thinking behind those. The leader concludes with asking the person who owned this case for their key learnings.

Common Interest Discussion

This is the third item on the agenda. The leader sets it up by asking everyone to share their perspective on a specific topic of interest to all present, and then the group has an open conversation. This format generates a lot of active participation.

Session Close

The leader invites participants to each share something they will use from the day's conversations.

Seven-Eyed Model Questions and Reflections

There are lists of questions one can ask under each of the levels of the seven-eyed model. I've included a sampling of the ones that I have found particularly helpful. The list here uses, as an example, the topic of contracting: the presenter is curious about the conversations (and contract obligations) when a client says they want to leave the organization.

- Eye 1: Client and their context:
    - What are the roots of all this attitude, intensity, and language?
- Eye 2: Coach's interventions:
    - How is your coaching agreement helping or hurting your management of the boundaries in this issue?

- Eye 3: Coach-client relationship:
    - How challenging is it to build a relationship with someone who displays these behaviors?
    - What metaphor captures your relationship with your client?
- Eye 4: Coach self-awareness:
    - How is it for you when your values are *not* reciprocated?
    - Is there a long-term versus short-term perception shift that could help reframe the dilemma?
    - What would it take to have fun and bring your curiosity back into play?
- Eye 5: Supervisor-to-coach relationship:
    - Who says we have to be great with all our clients?
    - Do you appreciate how hard this is for all of us?
- Eye 6: Supervisor self-reflection:
    - I am having a visceral reaction and can feel my heart beating faster. Is this you too?
    - What could I do to more deeply connect with your issues?
- Eye 7: Wider context:
    - What are the external system considerations, and how does this company's culture add unique stressors?

Coaching Post-session Reflection

How well did I meet the contracted deliverables?

- What did the coach (the client) gain today?
- What feedback did I receive from the coach?
- Any areas for more attention?

How well do I think I did, against my standards?

- Did I show up as I intended?
- Did I work on what I wanted to work on? How did it go?
- How did my comments map against Hawkins's seven-eyed model?
- Anything to bring into my own supervision?

SUPERVISION CHAIN GROUP

This model of group supervision is the most restrictive in terms of membership; entry is restricted to graduates of a coaching supervision certification program. The learning objective is to deepen our skills as supervisors and to learn how it feels to be supervised.

Intention

The idea is to provide a long-term forum for applying and deepening our coaching supervision skills. It is also to deepen our capacity for authentic and open discussions of the things that are important in our supervision work.

Logistics

Dyads of certified supervisors agree to serve in both a supervisor and a supervisee role for between one and three hours per quarter. Matched participants are set up on an Excel spreadsheet, and dyads change quarterly. In the following spreadsheet, you can see how the supervisee shifts up one cell each quarter. The supervisee must contact the supervisor to schedule their meetings. In any quarter, each member participates in two different dyads—one in the supervisor capacity and one in the supervisee capacity.

Supervisor	Supervisee (this quarter)	Supervisee (next quarter)
Person 1	Person 2	Person 3
Person 2	Person 3	Person 4
Person 3	Person 4	Person 5
Person 4	Person 5	Person 6
Person 5	Person 6	Person 7
Person 6	Person 7	Person 8
Person 7	Person 8	Person 9
Person 8	Person 9	Person 10
Person 9	Person 10	Person 1
Person 10	Person 1	Person 2

Membership Changes

Membership changes can occur only at the quarterly meetings and are restricted to members of the same certification class cohort. New members require 100% group approval. While our group had ten members, Clutterbuck provides examples with far fewer members.[5]

Dyad Contracting

Each supervisee is expected to present one or two cases to gain supervision on an issue or challenge. The definition of *supervision* provided in Chapter 7 defines the duties of both parties: "a safe space for reflective dialogue with a practicing supervisor, supporting the supervisee's practice, development, and well-being."[6]

Quarterly Meetings

The whole group meets quarterly to share experiences and to provide opportunities for short teaching segments. Facilitation rotates each quarter. A typical agenda for a one-hour quarterly meeting includes:

- Roundtable on important things going on in our lives, supervision, and professional practice
- Open discussion on what we find helps or hinders our effectiveness as supervisors
- Sharing ideas on building our supervision practice
- Sharing how being in this supervision group helps us learn and grow
- Seeking of a volunteer for next quarter's facilitator and schedule

Notes

Chapter One

1. S. Sherman and A. Freas, "The Wild West of Executive Coaching," *Harvard Business Review*, November 2004, pp. 82–90.
2. B. O. Underhill, K. McAnally, and J. J. Koriath, *Executive Coaching for Results*, San Francisco: Barrett-Koehler, 2007.
3. Ibid.
4. J. Elliott, *Requisite Organization: A Total System for Effective Managerial Organization and Managerial Leadership for the 21st Century*, Arlington, VA: Carson Hall, 1998; D. Katz and R. L. Kahn, *The Social Psychology of Organizations*, 2nd ed., Hoboken, NJ: Wiley, 1978; H. Mintzberg, *The Nature of Managerial Work*, New York: HarperCollins College, 1973.
5. L. A. Steelman, P. E. Levy, and A. F. Snell, "The Feedback Environment Scale: Construct Definition, Measurement, and Validation," *Educational and Psychological Measurement*, 64 (2004), pp. 165–184.
6. K. McAnally, L. Abrams, M. J. Asmus, and T. Hildebrandt, "Global Coaching Supervision: A Study of the Perceptions and Practices Around the World," 2020, https://coachingsupervisionresearch.org/wp-content/uploads/2020/02/Global_Coaching_Supervision_Report_FINAL.pdf.
7. T. Sechrest and T. M. Middelberg, "Using the RFDA Model as a Tool for Developing Ethical Leadership," *Perspectives in Business*, 4:1 (2007), pp. 23–27.

Chapter Two

1. P. Zeus and S. Skiffington, *Behavioral Coaching*, New York: McGraw-Hill, 2003.

2. P. Lencioni, *The Five Dysfunctions of a Team: A Leadership Fable,* San Francisco: Jossey-Bass, 2002, p. 195.

3. F. Fukuyama, *Trust: The Social Virtues and the Creation of Prosperity*, New York: Free Press, 1996.

4. S. M. R. Covey, S. R. Covey, and R. R. Merrill, *The Speed of Trust*, New York: Free Press, 2008.

5. Ibid., p. 13.

6. Ibid.

7. C. Argyris and D. A. Schön, *Theory in Practice: Increasing Professional Effectiveness*, San Francisco: Jossey-Bass, 1978.

8. L. G. Bolman and T. E. Deal, *Reframing Organizations: Artistry, Choice, and Leadership,* 4th ed., San Francisco: Jossey-Bass, 2008.

9. Ibid., pp. 170–171.

10. L. Powers, *The Trouble with Thinking: Adventures in Self Smarts, Book One*, Bloomington, NY: iUniverse Star, 2010.

11. Ibid., p. 34.

12. J. Mezirow, *Fostering Critical Reflection in Adulthood*, San Francisco: Jossey-Bass, 1990; D. Schön, *Educating the Reflective Practitioner*, San Francisco: Jossey-Bass, 1987; S. Brookfield, *Understanding and Facilitating Adult Learning*, Buckingham, UK: McGraw-Hill Open University Press, 1986; J. Mezirow, *Transformative Dimensions of Adult Learning*, San Francisco: Jossey-Bass, 1991.

13. D. Clutterbuck, C. Whitaker, and M. Lucas, *Coaching Supervision: A Practical Guide for Supervisee*, New York: Routledge, 2016; J. Hay, *Reflective Practice and Supervision for Coaches*, Berkshire, UK: McGraw-Hill Open University Press, 2007; E. Cox, "An Adult Learning Approach to Coaching," in D. R. Strober and A. M. Grant, eds., *Evidence Based Coaching Handbook*, Hoboken, NJ: John Wiley and Sons, 2006.

14. L. West and M. Milan, *The Reflecting Glass: Professional Coaching for Leadership Development*, Basingstoke, UK: Palgrave Macmillan, 2001, pp. 7–8.

15. K. McAnally, L. Abrams, M. J. Asmus, and T. H. Hildebrandt, "Coaching Supervision," in T. H. Hildebrandt, F. Campone, K. Norwood, and E. J. Ostrowski, eds., *Innovations in Leadership Coaching: Research and Practice*, Santa Barbara, CA: Fielding University Press, 2020, p. 407.

16. D. Kahneman and A. Tversky, *Choices, Values, and Frames*, Cambridge, UK: Cambridge University Press, 2000.

17. D. R. Ilgen, C. D. Fisher, and M. S. Taylor, "Consequences of Individual Feedback of Behavior in Organizations," *Journal of Applied Psychology*, 64:4 (1979), pp. 349–371; S. J. Ashford and A. S. Tsui, "Self-Regulation for Managerial Effectiveness: The Role of Active Feedback Seeking," *Academy of Management Journal*, 34:2 (1991), pp. 251–280; S. J. Ashford, "The Role of Feedback Seeking in Individual Adaptation," *Academy of Management Journal*, 29 (1986), pp. 465–487.

18. A. Church, "Managerial Self-Awareness in High-Performing Individuals in Organizations," *Journal of Applied Psychology*, 82:2 (1997), pp. 281–292.

19. D. Goleman, *Emotional Intelligence: Why It Can Matter More Than IQ*, 10th ed., New York: Bantam, 2006.

20. Atul Gawande, "Personal Best," *New Yorker*, October 3, 2011, http://www.newyorker.com/reporting/2011/10/03/111003fa_fact_gawande (accessed November 9, 2011).

21. C. Argyris, *Overcoming Organizational Defenses: Facilitating Organizational Learning*, Boston: Allyn and Bacon, 1990.

22. D. R. Ilgen, C. D. Fisher, and M. S. Taylor, "Consequences of Individual Feedback on Behavior in Organizations," *Journal of Applied Psychology*, 64:4 (1979), pp. 349–371.

23. E. W. Morrison and R. J. Bies, "Impression Management in the Feedback-Seeking Process: A Literature Review and Research Agenda," *Academy of Management Review*, 16:3 (1991), pp. 522–541.

24. Ashford and Tsui, "Self-Regulation for Managerial Effectiveness."

25. G. B. Graen and M. Uhl-Bien, "Relationship-Based Approach to Leadership: Development of Leader-Member Exchange (LMX) Theory over 25 Years: Applying a Multi-level Multi-domain Perspective," *Leadership Quarterly*, 6:2 (1995), pp. 219–247.

26. J. M. Maslyn and M. Uhl-Bien, "Leader-Member Exchange and Its Dimensions: Effects of Self-Other's Effort on Relationship Quality," *Journal of Applied Psychology*, 86 (2001), pp. 697–708.

27. Graen and Uhl-Bien, "Relationship-Based Approach to Leadership."

28. S. W. Porges, *The Polyvagal Theory: Neurophysiological Foundations of Emotions, Attachment, Communication, and Self-Regulation*, New York: Norton, 2011.

29. T. M. Middelberg, "The Relationship Between Leader Behaviors and Job Satisfaction and Collective Efficacy," unpublished dissertation, University of Texas at Austin, 1999.

30. M. B. Eberly et al., "Beyond Internal and External: A Dyadic Theory of Relational Attributions," *Academy of Management Review*, 36:4 (2011), pp. 731–753.

31. L. A. Steelman, P. E. Levy, and A. F. Snell, "The Feedback Environment Scale: Construct Definition, Measurement, and Validation," *Educational and Psychological Measurement*, 64 (2004), pp. 165–184.

32. K. Lewin, *Resolving Social Conflicts and Field Theory in Social Science*, Washington, DC: American Psychological Association, 1997.

33. Y. M. Agazarian, *Systems-Centered Therapy for Groups*, London: Karnac Books, 2004.

34. W. Bridges, *Managing Transitions: Making the Most of Change*, 3rd ed., Cambridge, MA: Da Capo, 2009; E. Kubler-Ross, *On Death and Dying*, New York: Routledge, 1969; J. P. Kotter, *Leading Change*, Boston: Harvard Business School Press, 1996; K. Lewin, *The Complete Social Scientist: A Kurt Lewin Reader*, ed. M. Gold, Washington, DC: American Psychological Association, 1999; J. O. Prochaska, J. C. Norcross, and C. C. DiClemente, *Changing for Good: A Revolutionary Six-Stage Program for Overcoming Bad Habits and Moving Your Life Positively Forward*, New York: William Morrow, 1994.

35. M. Goldsmith, *What Got You Here Won't Get You There*, New York: Hyperion, 2007.

36. A. Beisser, "The Paradoxical Theory of Change" [1970], in J. Fagan and L. L. Shepherd, eds., *Gestalt Therapy Now*, Gouldsboro, ME: Gestalt Journal Press, 2006, pp. 77–80.

37. Prochaska, Norcross, and DiClemente, *Changing for Good.*

38. B. O. Underhill, K. McAnally, and J. J. Koriath, *Executive Coaching for Results: The Definitive Guide to Developing Organizational Leaders*, San Francisco: Berrett-Koehler, 2007.

39. J. L. Sparr and S. Sonnentag, "Feedback Environment and Well-Being at Work: The Mediating Role of Personal Control and Feelings of Helplessness," *European Journal of Work and Organizational Psychology*, 17:3 (2008), pp. 388–412.

40. S. E. Finn, *In Our Clients' Shoes: Theory and Techniques of Therapeutic Assessment*, Mahwah, NJ: Erlbaum, 2007.

Chapter Three

1. T. M. Middelberg, "The Relationship Between Leader Behaviors and Job Satisfaction and Collective Efficacy," unpublished dissertation, University of Texas at Austin, 1999.

2. R. S. Kaplan, "Top Executives Need Feedback—Here's How They Can Get It," *McKinsey Quarterly*, 4 (2011), pp. 60–71.

3. K. Lewin, *Resolving Social Conflicts and Field Theory in Social Science*, Washington, DC: American Psychological Association, 1997.

4. M. Buckingham and D. O. Clifton, *Now, Discover Your Strengths*, New York: Free Press, 2001; D. L. Cooperrider, D. Whitney, and J. M. Stavros, *Appreciative Inquiry Handbook,* 2nd ed., Brunswick, OH: Crown Custom, 2008.
5. W. R. Miller and S. Rollnik, *Motivational Interviewing: Preparing People for Change*, 2nd ed., New York: Guilford Press, 2002.
6. Y. Boshyk, ed., *Business-Driven Action Learning: Global Best Practices*, New York: St. Martin's, 2000; R. O. Brinkerhoff, *The Success Case Method*, San Francisco: Berrett-Koehler, 2003; M. J. Marquardt, *Action Learning in Action: Transforming Problems and People for World-Class Organizational Learning*, Palo Alto, CA: Davis-Black, 1999; W. J. Rothwell, *The Action Learning Guidebook*, San Francisco: Jossey-Bass/Pfeiffer, 1999; K. E. Watkins and V. J. Marsick, *Sculpting the Learning Organization: Lessons in the Art and Science of Systemic Change*, San Francisco: Jossey-Bass, 1993.
7. See the Center for Creative Leadership's website, at http://www.ccl.org.
8. Brinkerhoff, *The Success Case Method.*

Chapter Four

1. International Coaching Federation, "ICF Core Competencies," https://coachingfederation.org/core-competencies (accessed February 18, 2022).
2. J. M. Kouzes and B. Z. Pozner, *The Leadership Challenge*, 4th ed., San Francisco: Jossey-Bass, 2008; W. Bennis, *Why Leaders Can't Lead: The Unconscious Conspiracy Continues*, San Francisco: Jossey-Bass, 1997.
3. K. Lewin, *Resolving Social Conflicts and Field Theory in Social Science*, Washington, DC: American Psychological Association, 1997.
4. Y. M. Agazarian, *Systems-Centered Therapy for Groups*, London: Karnac Books, 2004.
5. J. H. Zenger and J. R. Folkman, *The Extraordinary Leader: Turning Good Managers into Great Leaders*, New York: McGraw-Hill, 2009.
6. D. Goleman, *Emotional Intelligence: Why It Can Matter More Than IQ*, New York: Bantam, 1995; D. Goleman and R. Boyatzis, "Social Intelligence and the Biology of Leadership," *Harvard Business Review*, September 2008, pp. 74–81; D. J. Siegel, *Mindsight: The New Science of Personal Transformation*, New York: Random House, 2010.
7. See the international Coach Federation's website, at http://www.coachfederation.org.
8. F. Moen and R. A. Federici, "Perceptions of Coach Competence and Perceived Need Satisfaction: Assessing a Norwegian Coach Competence Scale," *International Journal of Coaching in Organizations*, 8:32 (2011), pp. 124–138;

D. Goldvarg, P. Mathews, and N. Perel, *Professional Coaching Competencies: The Complete Guide*, Arroyo Grande, CA: Executive College Press, 2018; J. Rogers, *Coaching Skills: The Definitive Guide to Being a Coach*, 4th ed., New York: Open University Press, 2016; D. Rock and L. J. Page, *Coaching with the Brain in Mind: Foundations for Practice*, Hoboken, NJ: John Wiley and Sons, 2009; T. H. Hildebrand, F. Campone, K. Norwood, and E. J. Ostrowski, eds., *Innovations in Leadership Coaching: Research and Practice*, Santa Barbara, CA: Fielding Graduate University, 2020.

9. S. E. Finn, *In Our Clients' Shoes: Theory and Techniques of Therapeutic Assessment*, Mahwah, NJ: Erlbaum, 2007.
10. E. H. Schein and P. A. Schein, *Humble Inquiry: The Gentile Art of Asking Instead of Telling*, 2nd ed., Oakland, CA: Berrett-Koehler, 2021.
11. W. Bridges, *Managing Transitions: Making the Most of Change*, 3rd ed., Cambridge, MA: Da Capo, 2009; E. Kubler-Ross, *On Death and Dying*, New York: Routledge, 1969; J. P. Kotter, *Leading Change*, Boston: Harvard Business School Press, 1969; K. Lewin, *The Complete Social Scientist: A Kurt Lewin Reader*, ed. M. Gold, Washington, DC: American Psychological Association, 1999; J. O. Prochaska, J. C. Norcross, and C. C. DiClemente, *Changing for Good: A Revolutionary Six-Stage Program for Overcoming Bad Habits and Moving Your Life Positively Forward*, New York: William Morrow, 1994.
12. G. O'Donovan, *The Corporate Culture Handbook: How to Plan, Implement, and Measure a Successful Cultural Change Program*, Dublin: Liffey Press, 2006; R. Connors and T. Smith, *Journey to the Emerald City: Achieve a Competitive Edge by Creating a Culture of Accountability*, New York: Prentice-Hall, 1999.

Chapter Five

1. T. Kemp, "Coach Self-Management: The Foundation of Coaching Effectiveness," in D. B. Drake, D. Bennan, and K. Gortz, eds., *Philosophy and Practice of Coaching: Insights and Issues for a New Era*, West Sussex, UK: Wiley, 2008, p. 28.
2. R. M. Kramer, "Organizational Trust: Progress and Promise in Theory and Research," in R. M. Kramer, ed., *Organizational Trust: A Reader*, Oxford, UK: Oxford University Press, 2006.
3. R. Elliott, J. C. Watson, R. N. Goldman, and L. S. Greenberg, *Learning Emotion-Focused Therapy: The Process-Experiential Approach to Change*, Washington, DC: American Psychological Association, 2004.
4. Y. M. Agazarian, *Systems-Centered Therapy for Groups*, London: Karnac Books, 2004.
5. C. Argyris and D. A. Schön, *Organizational Learning II: Theory, Method, and Practice*, New York: Addison-Wesley, 1995.

6. T. Gilovic, D. Griffin, and D. Kahneman, eds., *Heuristics and Biases: The Psychology of Intuitive Judgment*, Cambridge, UK: Cambridge University Press, 2002.
7. Peter M. Senge, Charlotte Roberts, Richard B. Ross, Bryan J. Smith, and Art Kleiner, *The Fifith Discipline Fieldbook: Strategies and Tools for Building a Learning Organization*, New York: Doubleday, 1994.
8. T. Gilovic, D. Griffin, and D. Kahneman, eds., *Heuristics and Biases: The Psychology of Intuitive Judgment*, Cambridge, UK: Cambridge University Press, 2002.
9. J. Mesirow and Associates, *Fostering Critical Reflection in Adulthood: A Guide to Transformative and Emancipatory Learning*, San Francisco: Jossey-Bass, 1990.
10. C. K. Germer, *The Mindful Path to Self-Compassion: Freeing Yourself from Destructive Thoughts and Emotions*, New York: Guilford Press, 2009; C. K. Germer, R. D. Siegel, and P. R. Fulton, eds., *Mindfulness and Psychotherapy*, New York: Guilford Press, 2005.
11. D. J. Siegel, *The Mindful Brain: Reflection and Attunement in the Cultivation of Well-Being*, New York: Norton, 2007.
12. Kemp, "Coach Self-Management," pp. 41–42.
13. Ibid., p. 40.
14. Germer, *The Mindful Path to Self-Compassion,* p. 25.
15. J. Fixx, *Jim Fixx's Second Book of Running*, New York: Random House, 1980.
16. K. D. Neff, *Self-Compassion: Stop Beating Yourself Up and Leave Insecurity Behind*, New York: William Morrow, 2011.
17. B. L. Halpern and K. Lubar, *Executive Presence*, New York: Gotham Books, 2003.
18. R. K. Greenleaf, *Servant Leadership,* Mahwah, NJ: Paulist Press, [1977] 2002.
19. W. Bennis, *On Becoming a Leader*, New York: Addison-Wesley, 1989.
20. R. W. Emerson, *Self-Reliance*, Greensboro, NC: Empire Books, 2011, p. 2.
21. R. S. Moxley, *Leadership and Spirit*, San Francisco: Jossey-Bass, 2000.
22. P. Block, *Flawless Consulting*, San Diego: Pfeiffer, 2001.
23. P. Jarvis, *The Practitioner-Researcher*, San Francisco: Jossey-Bass, 1999.
24. A. Rubin and E. Babbie, *Research Methods of Social Work*, 2nd ed., Pacific Grove, CA: Brooks/Cole, 1993.
25. M. J. Gleb, *How to Think Like Leonardo da Vinci*, New York: Delacorte, 1998; J. Gleick, *Genius: The Life and Science of Richard Feynman*, New York: Vintage, 1993; Harvard Business Essentials, *Managing Creativity and Innovation*, Boston: Harvard Business School Publishing, 2003; T. Hurson, *Think Better: An Innovator's Guide to Productive Thinking*, New York: McGraw-Hill, 2007.

26. D. Campbell, R. Draper, and C. Huffington, *A Systemic Approach to Consultation*, London: Karnac Books, 1989.

27. E. R. Shapiro and A. W. Carr, *Lost in Familiar Places: Creating New Connections Between the Individual and Society*, New Haven, CT: Yale University Press, 1991.

Chapter Six

1. S. Dening, *The Leader's Guide to Storytelling*, San Francisco: Jossey-Bass, 2005; A. Simmons, *The Story Factor: Secrets of Influence from the Art of Storytelling*, Cambridge, MA: Perseus, 2001.

2. J. R. Hackman, *Leading Teams: Setting the Stage for Great Performances*, Boston: Harvard Business School Press, 2002.

3. P. Drucker, *The Concept of the Corporation*, New York: John Day, 1946.

4. D. Clutterbuck, C. Whitaker, and M. Lucas, *Coaching Supervision: A Practical Guide for Supervisees*, New York: Routledge, 2016, p. 182.

5. D. L. Cooperrider, D. Whitney, and J. M. Stavros, *Appreciative Inquiry Handbook*, 2nd ed., Brunswick, OH: Crown Custom, 2008.

6. Y. Boshyk, ed., *Business Driven Action Learning: Global Best Practices*, New York: St. Martin's, 2000; M. J. Marquardt, *Action Learning in Action: Transforming Problems and People for World-Class Organizational Learning*, Palo Alto, CA: Davis-Black, 1999; W. J. Rothwell, *The Action Learning Guidebook*, San Francisco: Jossey-Bass/Pfeiffer, 1999; K. E. Watkins and V. J. Marsick, *Sculpting the Learning Organization: Lessons in the Art and Science of Systemic Change*, San Francisco: Jossey-Bass, 1993.

Chapter Seven

1. K. McAnally, L. Abrams, M. J. Asmus, and T. Hildebrandt, "Global Coaching Supervision: A Study of the Perceptions and Practices Around the World," 2020, https://coachingsupervisionresearch.org/wp-content/uploads/2020/02/Global_Coaching_Supervision_Report_FINAL.pdf; personal communications with Damian Goldvarg of Goldvarg Consulting Group (https://goldvargconsulting.com/executive-coaching/coaching-supervision-certification/), January 2017.

2. M. J. Marquardt, *Action Learning in Action: Transforming Problems and People for World-Class Organizational Learning*, Palo Alto, CA: Davis-Black, 1999; J. Mezirow and Associates, *Fostering Critical Reflection in Adulthood: A Guide to Transformative and Emancipatory Learning*, San Francisco: Jossey-Bass, 1991.

3. M. S. Knowles, E. F. Holton III, and R. A. Swanson, *The Adult Learner: The Definitive Classic in Adult Education and Human Resource Development*, 8th ed., London: Routledge, 2015.

4. P. J. Palmer, *Let Your Life Speak: Listening to the Voice of Vocation*, San Francisco: Jossey-Bass, 2000.
5. D. Silsbee, *Presence-Based Coaching*, San Francisco: Jossey-Bass, 2008.
6. EMCC Global, "Definition," https://www.emccglobal.org/leadership-development/supervision/definition/ (accessed November 5, 2021).
7. P. Hawkins and R. Shohet, *Supervision in the Helping Professions*, 4th ed., New York: McGraw-Hill Open University Press, 2012; P. Hawkins and N. Smith, *Coaching, Mentoring and Organizational Consultancy: Supervision, Skills and Development*, 2nd ed., New York: McGraw-Hill Open University Press, 2013; P. Hawkins and E. Turner, *Systemic Coaching: Delivering Value Beyond the Individual*, New York: Routledge, 2019.
8. K. Lewin, *The Complete Social Scientist: A Kurt Lewin Reader*, ed. M. Gold, Washington, DC: American Psychological Association, 1999.
9. Y. M. Agazarian, *Systems-Centered Therapy for Group*, London: Karnac Books, 2004.
10. E. W. Morrison and R. J. Bies, "Impression Management in the Feedback-Seeking Process: A Literature Review and Research Agenda," *Academy of Management Review*, 16:3 (1991), pp. 522–541; J. R. Folkman, *The Power of Feedback*, New York: John Wiley and Sons, 2006; D. Stone, B. Patton, and S. Heen, *Difficult Conversation: How to Discuss What Matters Most*, 10th ed., New York: Penguin Books, 2010.
11. S. J. Ashford and A. S. Tsui, "Self-Regulation for Managerial Effectiveness: The Role of Active Feedback Seeking," *Academy of Management Journal*, 34:2 (1991), pp. 251–280.
12. Atul Gawande, "Personal Best," *New Yorker*, October 3, 2011, http://www.newyorker.com/reporting/2011/10/03/111003fa_fact_gawande.
13. Hawkins and Smith, *Coaching, Mentoring and Organizational Consultancy*.
14. McAnally et al., "Global Coaching Supervision."
15. J. Hays, *Reflective Practice and Supervision for Coaches*, Berkshire, UK: McGraw-Hill Open University Press, 2007.
16. D. Clutterbuck, C. Whitaker, and M. Lucas, *Coaching Supervision: A Practical Guide for Supervisees*, New York: Routledge, 2016.
17. N. Hill, *Think and Grow Rich*, New York: Penguin, 2005.
18. H. Cochrane and T. Newton, *Supervision and Coaching: Growth and Learning in Professional Practice*, New York: Routledge, 2018; Hawkins and Shohet, *Supervision in the Helping Professions*; T. Bachkirova, P. Jackson, and D. Clutterbuck, *Coaching and Mentoring Supervision: Theory and Practice*, New York: McGraw-Hill Open University Press, 2011; Hawkins and Turner, *Systemic Coaching*; Hay, *Reflective Practice and Supervision for Coaches*; Hawkins and Smith, *Coaching, Mentoring and Organizational Consultancy*.

Chapter Eight

1. M. Biquet, *Ethical Dilemmas in Coaching Today: A Professional Dilemmas Survey*, Brussels, Belgium: EMCC Global, 2020.
2. D. A. Schön, *The Reflective Practitioner: How Professionals Think in Action*, New York: Basic Books, 1983, p. 17.
3. K. S. Kitchener, "Intuition, Critical Evaluation and Ethical Principles: The Foundation for Ethical Decisions in Counseling Psychology," *Counseling Psychologist*, 12 (2000), pp. 43–55; R. Kidder, *How Good People Make Tough Choices*, New York: Fireside, 1996; J. B. Ciulla, *Ethics, the Heart of Leadership*, 3rd ed., Santa Barbara, CA: Praeger, 2014.
4. International Coaching Federation, "ICF Code of Ethics," https://coachingfederation.org/ethics/code-of-ethics (accessed October 5, 2021).
5. Global Code of Ethics, "About the Global Code of Ethics for Coaches, Mentors, and Supervisors," https://www.globalcodeofethics.org/ (accessed November 15, 2021).
6. I. Iordanou, R. Hawley, and C. Iordanou, *Values and Ethics in Coaching*, London: Sage, 2017, p. 25.
7. I. Nonaka and H. Takeuchi, *The Knowledge-Creating Company: How Japanese Companies Create the Dynamics of Innovation*, New York: Oxford University Press, 1995.
8. J. R. Rest, *Moral Development: Advances in Research and Theory*, New York: Praeger, 1986.
9. T. Sechrest and T. M. Middelberg, "Using the RFDA Model as a Tool for Developing Ethical Leadership," *Perspectives in Business*, 4:1 (2007), pp. 23–27.
10. M. Knowles, E. F. Holton III, and R. A. Swanson, *The Adult Learner: The Definitive Classic in Adult Education and Human Development*, 8th ed., London: Routledge, 2015; J. Mezirow, *Fostering Critical Reflection in Adulthood: A Guide to Transformative and Emancipatory Learning*, San Francisco: Jossey-Bass, 1990; Schön, *The Reflective Practitioner*; D. A. Kolb, *Experiential Learning: Experience as the Source of Learning and Development*, Englewood Cliffs, NJ: Prentice-Hall, 1984; G. Collier, "Learning Moral Judgment in Higher Education," *Studies in Higher Education*, 18:3 (1993), pp. 287–298.
11. J. B. Ciulla, *Ethics, the Heart of Leadership*, 3rd ed., Santa Barbara, CA: Praeger, 2014; Iordanou, Hawley, and Iordanou, *Values and Ethics in Coaching*; P. Williams and S. K. Anderson, *Law and Ethics in Coaching: How to Solve and Avoid Difficult Problems in Your Practice*, Hoboken, NJ: John Wiley and Sons, 2006.
12. International Coaching Federation, "ICF Code of Ethics."

13. N. E. Ruely and M. E. Schweitzer, "In the Moment: The Effect of Mindfulness on Ethical Decision Making," *Journal of Business Ethics*, 95 (February 2011), pp. 73–87; S. Gellor and L. S. Greenberg, *Therapeutic Presence: A Mindful Approach to Effective Therapy*, Washington, DC: American Psychological Association, 2012.
14. D. Clutterbuck, foreword to I. Iordanou, R. Hawley, and C. Iordanou, *Values and Ethics in Coaching*, p. xi.
15. Biquet, *Ethical Dilemmas in Coaching Today*, p. 18.
16. International Coaching Federation, "ICF Code of Ethics."
17. A. Maxwell, "Supervising the Internal Coach," in T. Bachkirova, P. Jackson, and D. Clutterbuck, eds., *Coaching and Mentoring Supervision: Theory and Practice*, London: Open University Press, 2011.
18. S. Western, *Coaching and Mentoring: A Critical Text*, Los Angeles: Sage, 2012, p. 204.
19. International Coaching Federation, "Leading the Global Advancement of the Coaching Profession," https://coachingfederation.org/about (accessed February 18, 2022).
20. D. Goldvarg, P. Mathews, and N. Perel, *Professional Coaching Competencies: The Complete Guide*, Arroyo Grande, CA: Executive College Press, 2018.
21. J. Mezirow and Associates, *Fostering Critical Reflection in Adulthood: A Guide to Transformative and Emancipatory Learning*, San Francisco: Jossey-Bass, 1991; M. S. Knowles, E. F. Holton III, and R. A. Swanson, *The Adult Learner: The Definitive Classic in Adult Education and Human Resource Development*, 8th ed., London: Routledge, 2015; D. A. Kolb, *Experiential Learning: Experience as the Source of Learning and Development*, Englewood Cliffs, NJ: Prentice-Hall, 1984.

Appendix F

1. N. Hill, *Think and Grow Rich*, New York: Penguin, 2005.
2. The model was developed in 2016 through the collaborative efforts of Edna Harris, Kelley Russell-DuVarney, Sherry Lowry, and Ted Middelberg.
3. K. Pinder, "Group Supervision," in T. Bachkirova, P. Jackson, and D. Clutterbuck, eds., *Coaching and Mentoring Supervision: Theory and Practice*, New York: McGraw-Hill Open University Press, 2011, pp. 196–204.
4. P. Hawkins and G. Schwenk, "The Seven-Eyed Model of Coaching Supervision," in T. Bachkirova, P. Jackson, and D. Clutterbuck, eds., *Coaching and Mentoring Supervision: Theory and Practice*, New York: McGraw-Hill Open University Press, 2011, pp. 28–40; Pinder, "Group Supervision"; P. Hawkins and N. Smith, *Coaching, Mentoring and Organizational Consultancy: Supervision, Skills and Development*, 2nd ed., New York: McGraw-Hill Open University Press, 2013.

5. D. Clutterbuck, C. Whitaker, and M. Lucas, *Coaching Supervision: A Practical Guide for Supervisees*, New York: Routledge, 2016.
6. EMCC Global, "Definition," https://www.emccglobal.org/leadership-development/supervision/definition/ (accessed November 5, 2021).

Index

A

B

C

D

S

T

U

V

W

Z

About the Author

Ted Middelberg is founder of Transformational Executive Coaching LLC, a consultancy specializing in helping leaders to achieve more. His track record of success includes working with leaders at some of the world's largest companies. He brings a wealth of knowledge from his experience as a financial executive and a leadership development expert in the high-tech industry. He has a lifelong commitment to the role of researcher-practitioner. He earned his bachelors at Brown University, his MBA at The Ohio State University, and his Ed.D., in 1999, at The University of Texas. Ted has certificates as an executive coach and as a coaching supervisor. He teaches a course on coaching at St. Edward's University in the Leadership in Higher Education doctoral program. He resides in Austin, Texas.